# Feasts of Veg

*Vibrant Vegetarian Recipes for Gatherings*

———

Nina Olsson

An Hachette UK Company
www.hachette.co.uk

First published in Great Britain in 2018 by
Kyle Books, an imprint of Kyle Cathie Ltd
Carmelite House
50 Victoria Embankment
London EC4Y 0DZ
www.kylebooks.co.uk

This edition published in 2018

Distributed in the US by Hachette Book Group, 1290 Avenue of the
Americas, 4th and 5th Floors, New York, NY 10104

Distributed in Canada by Canadian Manda Group, 664 Annette St.,
Toronto, Ontario, Canada M6S 2C8

ISBN: 978 1 90948 788 8

Photographer, Stylist and Designer: Nina Olsson
Assisting stylists: Sarah Cheikh, Nova Olsson, Bensimon
Van Leyen, Fleur Schouten, and Santouscha Tjietaman
Project Editor: Sophie Allen
Copy Editor: Jo Richardson
Editorial assistant: Sarah Kyle
Production: Nic Jones, Gemma John and Lisa Pinnell

10 9 8 7 6 5 4 3 2 1

# Contents

Introduction 4

Small Bites 8

Midsummer Feast 38

Midwinter Feast 52

Celebration Salads 72

Hearty Meals 94

Sides and Sharing Dishes 118

Al Fresco 140

Plated 156

Sweet Endings 172

Index 188

Acknowledgments 192

# Sharing the Goodness

**This book is filled with** vegetarian recipes for dinners, gatherings, and parties. It's the kind of food I like to eat myself and to serve to friends and family. There's no more beautiful meal to share than a feast with vibrant vegetables, whether it's a golden roasted root gratin with mushrooms or a sparkling rainbow-colored salad. This book is about sharing good food, one of the most enjoyable things to do in life.

A great feast raises our spirits and you can actually say it's a form of wellness activity, so there's no need to feel indulgent for throwing the occasional party—you're sharing the goodness.

When I was too young to join in with my parents' dinner parties, my siblings and I would fall asleep to the muddled sound of laughter and music. I remember feeling excited, thinking this must be the best part of being a grown up, celebrating together, filling the house with food and friends. And when I pictured my older self, I saw myself cooking and hosting my own dinner parties. I still feel that excitement, especially when the cooking is done for the night and I can sit down with my guests at the table, enjoy a drink, and let the magic of the evening unfold.

My mother, who was a housewife in the seventies, preferred to put textiles and paint canvases before household duties, but she would go all out to make our celebrations memorable. One of the most cherished memories I have is from my seventh birthday, sitting at the head of a long table set on the grass with my friends, surrounded by lilac bushes in the high summer afternoon, with a layered strawberry cake, flowers, and lemonade. The love and effort my mom put into arranging this simple but unforgettable day, is my measuring stick for hosting today. My birthday happens to coincide with midsummer, which maybe adds to why I think it's the best holiday of the year. The feasts of our lives becomes memories in a timeline that we can see our own life stories through. At the heart of every feast there's a place, people, and good food.

Vegetables are the stars in this book and now is a really exciting time to be a vegetarian. The art of cooking vegetables is undergoing a renaissance, and there's virtually an army of creative chefs, authors, and bloggers all making a new style of vegetarianism happen. In my opinion, talking about vegetables and vegetarian food as a meat substitute, feels outdated today. It's not about "if" we should eat plant-based today, it's more a question about "how." And my own answer to that is to focus on flavor and take inspiration from world kitchens, to think outside the box and use techniques that can utilize the various textures and flavors of vegetables. The creative possibilities are vast. I can think of no better way to celebrate the future of food than by serving vegetables.

## Setting the scene

**A good party can** be a grand spectacle or as simple as a picnic in the park. In the end it's the spirit that we bring into it that matters. People, not furniture, make the party. A beautifully styled table with fine tableware and professional flower arrangements can be the stuff of lifelong memories, but it doesn't mean it's more enjoyable than a potluck gathering on the beach, grilling veggie burgers with the sun setting.

If you are hosting in your home, simply adding candlelight and flowers to the equation can set the right mood. Mixing new with old and borrowed tableware is always charming.

Taking the party outdoors, eating al fresco out in nature is fantastic: take chairs, tables, and (why not?) rugs, pouffes, and sofas to create a fabulous outdoor scene. Build a fire (in a safe manner) and hang lamps or light lanterns between trees.

# How to host a gathering

Gatherings are becoming increasingly casual in general—it's more about making sure there's a relaxed, welcoming atmosphere for the guests to enjoy, so don't stress. Forget about perfection or following strict etiquette!

So now you set a date and invite a number of people. Here are some pointers on how to throw a great dinner.

- **Being a relaxed host** is essential! Get organized, make a plan, and prepare as much as you can in advance.
- **Check in advance if any guests** have allergies or special diets and make adjustments accordingly.
- **Create atmosphere,** light candles, make a music play list, buy flowers, and rearrange furniture and declutter the space if it needs it.
- **Balance your menu,** and don't feed your guests too much bread, nibbles, or heavy starters if your main dish is the star dish on the menu. If everyone is getting full before you serve it, they won't appreciate your effort. Hunger is the best spice!
- **Make sure there's ice in the freezer** for drinks. And make sure there's enough glasses.
- **Have a wabi-sabi approach**: if something goes wrong, be light about it and move on.
- **Don't be overambitious.** Don't choose to cook several complicated dishes for one dinner, if you're cooking alone. Choose one more demanding dish to impress with and keep the rest simple. Or get someone to help.
- **It's always a good idea** to involve others for help, whether your partner or good friends. Delegate responsibility for dishes to others, or let them manage the music and bar, or have them making sure the dishwasher is emptied and filled between servings.
- **Also, make sure** guests are not excluded from conversation; if someone is being ignored, try to draw them into the dynamic.

## Get organized

Prepare what you can in advance so that you only need to finish the final steps of cooking a dish when guests have arrived. And remember that not every dish has to be homemade; it's perfectly fine to serve a quality chocolate, store-bought ice cream, or fruit after a main dish.

**Make a plan and shop in advance.**
**A few days ahead:**
Go through plates, tablecloths, glasses, and napkins and wash or replace as needed.
**Can be prepared a week ahead:**
Jams, confit, chutney, and ice cream
**Can be prepared a day ahead:**
Stews, curries, and soups. Store in the fridge and warm up just before serving. Leaving a stew to sit makes the flavors intensify and taste even better. Cold sauces, marinades, dressings, and nut and seaweed sprinkles can also be prepared a day ahead.
Cakes, bread, pizza dough, and cookies can be prepared hours or a day ahead. For layer cakes, assembly and spread on the filling and frosting just before serving.
Veggies that need to be roasted, fried, or grilled can be cut and marinated the day before.
Patties, sausages, and croquettes can be mixed and shaped and placed in the fridge a day ahead. Fry or grill just before serving.
Fresh pasta can be prepared a day ahead. Store in the fridge. Cook just before serving.
Syrups for cocktails can be mixed a day ahead.
**Can be prepared hours earlier on the same day:**
Salad can be made the same day. It tastes delicious the fresher it's made, so ideally no more than 2 to 3 hours before serving.

Before you start cooking, prepare your mise en place. Mise en place is a French expression for placing out all you need on your work surface before you start.

# How to use this book

All dishes can be freely combined to create a menu. I have mostly used organic ingredients where possible.

**Most recipes are sufficient** to serve four people; simply multiply amounts for bigger parties.

**Always taste the food** before serving and adjust with salt to taste, or if applicable, the amount of lemon juice, chile, or extra-virgin olive oil. I always salt carefully to allow guests to salt to their own taste.

**If you are on a sugar-free diet,** omit sugars from the recipe.

**If you don't use coconut products,** substitute with suitable replacement. Use another vegetable oil instead of coconut oil, and vegan or dairy cream instead of coconut milk.

**Soy sauce:** In this book I refer to soy sauce as Shoyu, the japanese name for soy sauce. Many soy sauces sold in supermarkets are made in China and often are made with artificial coloring and molasses, and are not fermented, which is the traditonal and more healthy way to consumer soy. Japanese soy is far more often fermented, so to be extra sure of getting a quality soy, or shoyu, shop at a natural foods store.

**Herbs:** Fresh delicate herbs like tarragon, basil, parsley, cilantro, and mint are interchangeable with each other but will alter the flavor. Bear in mind that mint adds quite a strong character. Sturdier herbs such as rosemary and thyme are easily interchangeable.

**Grains** are easily substituted with each other; adjust cooking times and amount of cooking liquid accordingly.

**Sweeteners:** I use honey or agave syrup as liquid sweeteners and coconut sugar or brown sugar where granulated sugar is required. I use the same sweeteners out of convenience. You can easily substitute honey and agave for maple syrup or other liquid sweeteners; if you use stevia, adjust the amount used accordingly.

**Hot sauces:** Hot sauces have different characteristics, and there's a variety used in the book. You can substitute other hot sauces and finely chopped fresh chiles.

**Vegan:** Where butter or ghee is listed, use vegetable oil instead. For dairy and egg products, use vegan substitutes. Suggestions are given with each recipe.

**Gluten-free:** Suggestions are given with each recipe.

## Substitutes

Most ingredients can be substituted with similar ingredients. As an example, if a recipe lists cavolo nero (black kale) as an ingredient you can easily substitute any other kale. Squashes and pumpkins are interchangeable, red onion with other onions, and so on.

> "A good cook is like a sorceress who dispenses happiness."
>
> ELSA SCHIAPARELLI

*Quick canapé ideas:
sliced cucumber topped
with red pesto and
red romaine salad
filled with hummus
and topped with
pomegranate seeds.*

# 1. SMALL BITES

These tempting nibbles and small servings are for serving to your guests
when they first arrive at your gathering, to satisfy their immediate hunger
but also to excite their appetites and expectations for what's to come.
Although these little dishes are designed to kick off the proceedings,
you can also mix and match them with dishes from other chapters
in the book, in either single or several servings.
Now let's get this party started!

# Okonomiyaki

MAKES 4 PANCAKES; SERVES 4

14 ounces radicchio or green cabbage, very finely shredded (or other finely shredded cabbage or finely grated vegetables—see headnote)

2 scallions, thinly sliced

2 tablespoons finely chopped pickled ginger, or 1 tablespoon ground ginger

3 tablespoons dashi or water

4 medium organic eggs, lightly beaten

2 cups all-purpose flour

1 teaspoon baking powder

salt, to taste

sesame or vegetable oil, for frying

OKONOMIYAKI SAUCE:

3 tablespoons Worcestershire sauce

3 tablespoons ketchup

3 tablespoons shoyu soy sauce or tamari

TO SERVE:

mayonnaise or Kewpie mayonnaise

furikake (see page 166 for homemade)

extra shredded cabbage or radicchio for topping

*Okonomiyaki* **translates from the Japanese literally as "how you want it," which means that this pancake recipe can be easily customized to your liking. Choose your favorite cabbage or other finely grated vegetables, like potato, beet, zucchini, and radishes.**

Mix together the ingredients for the onomiyaki sauce in a small bowl. For the pancakes, put the cabbage, scallions, ginger, dashi or water and beaten eggs in a large bowl and mix together until the vegetables are evenly coated with the egg. Sprinkle the flour and baking powder over the vegetable mixture and mix together, seasoning with salt.

Heat a skillet that has a lid over medium-high heat—the pancakes can easily burn, so take care that the pan doesn't get too hot. Drizzle the bottom of the pan with oil, then spoon in a quarter of the pancake mixture and swirl the pan to make a pancake about 6 inches in diameter. Fry for about a minute until it begins to firm. Cover the pan with the lid and continue cooking the pancake for 1 to 2 minutes until the underside is nicely browned. To flip the pancake, hold the lid firmly against the pan and invert the pan and lid together so that the pancake transfers to the lid. Lift the pan away and then carefully slide the pancake from the lid back into the pan with the browned side up. Fry for 1 to 2 minutes until the other side is golden brown, then slide onto a warmed plate. Repeat with the remainder of the pancake batter.

Serve the pancakes warm with the okonomiyaki sauce, mayonnaise, furikake, and extra shredded cabbage or radicchio for topping.

**VE** Opt for egg replacer, and vegan Worcestershire sauce and mayonnaise; make your own furikake (see page 166) or look for fish-free furikake if buying ready-made.
**GF** Check the contents of the baking powder to ensure that it's gluten-free; opt for gluten-free tamari.

# Hurricane Popcorn

SERVES 4

4 tablespoons (½ stick) butter, or
   3 tablespoons vegetable oil
½ teaspoon shoyu soy sauce or tamari
¼ cup popcorn kernels
salt, to taste (optional)

HURRICANE FURIKAKE SEASONING:

1 nori sheet, toasted and cut with scissors
   into very fine strips (plus a few extra
   strips, to garnish)
⅓ cup sesame seeds
2 tablespoons shoyu soy sauce or tamari
1½ teaspoons shichimi togarashi or red
   pepper flakes
1 tablespoon coconut sugar

**When I heard about this Hawaiian-style popcorn, I knew I would love it. Firstly, it fuses East and West by using the Japanese spice mix furikake, traditionally added to rice and other Japanese foods for a umami boost, to season good old popcorn. But to make it even more interesting, it also mixes savory and sweet flavors—always a winning combination—by adding a touch of coconut sugar to the seaweed-and-sesame-based furikake to give the popcorn a highly addictive funky flavor. Shichimi togarashi is a Japanese chile-based spice mix, which you can buy from well-stocked supermarkets, along with nori sheets, or from Asian supermarkets or online suppliers. Thanks, Hawaii!**

Put all the ingredients for the furikake seasoning in a food processor and process until well combined.

Prepare the popcorn shortly before serving to enjoy it at its best. Heat a large saucepan that has a tight-fitting lid over high heat. Add the butter or oil, soy sauce, and popcorn (if using butter, let it melt before adding the other ingredients), then shake the pan so that all the kernels are coated with the melted butter or oil. Cover the pan with the lid and cook until the sound of the popping has just stopped.

Transfer the popcorn to a bowl, add the furikake seasoning and salt to taste if you like, and toss to mix. It's now ready to serve.

**VE** Opt for vegetable oil.
**GF** Opt for gluten-free tamari.

### Pop it!

*There's been a huge trend of new creative popcorn brands offering exciting new flavors to taste. But of course nothing beats home-popped corn and you can easily create state of the art popcorn with various flavors at home. Try nutritional yeast, lingonberry powder, cinnamon, salty caramel chocolate, wasabi powder, za'atar, dill, or Parmesan for a delicious twist!*

*From the top left:*
*Hurricane Popcorn, furikake*
*seasoning, and natural popcorn*
*sprinkled with lingonberry powder*
*and coconut sugar.*

# Hot Eggplant Chips

**Feel like serving something a bit more adventurous than potato chips from a bag? These homemade eggplant alternatives are the perfect solution!**

———

SERVES 10

1 teaspoons shichimi togarashi

1 teaspoon salt, or to taste

4 small eggplants, thinly sliced lengthwise

toasted sesame oil, for brushing

2 small handfuls of panko breadcrumbs

RED PEPPER MISO DIP

1 roasted red pepper from a jar, drained

1 garlic clove, crushed

2 tablespoons red or brown miso

1 teaspoon sesame oil

2 tablespoons rice vinegar

water, to thin

salt, to taste

Preheat the oven to 350°F. Line two large baking sheets with parchment paper. Mix together the shichimi togarashi and salt. Arrange the eggplant slices in a single layer on the lined baking sheets. Brush with the toasted sesame oil and sprinkle with the spicy salt mix. Sprinkle with the panko breadcrumbs. Bake for 15 minutes, then flip the slices over and bake for 5 minutes more or until golden and crisp.

Meanwhile, to make the dip, blend all the dip ingredients together in a food processor. Add small amounts of water until you achieve the desired consistency. Adjust the seasoning with salt to taste. Serve immediately.

VE ✓

GF Chose gluten-free breadcrumbs or omit the panko breadcrumbs.

# Kale Chips and Lemony Cashew Cream

———

**These chips are featherlight and crispy. Add za'atar or another spice for extra interest. The lemony cashew cream is one of my all-time favorite dips, dairy-free and full of flavor.**

———

SERVES 4

LEMONY CASHEW CREAM:

3 tablespoons cashew butter

juice of ½ lemon

2 tablespoons extra-virgin olive oil

pinch of salt

1 garlic clove

1 teaspoon honey

3 tablespoons almond milk

KALE CRISPS:

1 pound savoy cabbage or cavolo nero (black kale), stemmed and leaves cut into small pieces

1 tablespoon olive oil, for baking

1½ tablespoons za'atar spice mix

pinch of salt

Preheat the oven to 400°F and line a baking sheet with parchment paper.

For the lemony cashew cream, mix all the cashew cream ingredients in a bowl and set aside until ready to serve.

For the chips, put the cabbage in a bowl. Drizzle with the olive oil and sprinkle with za'atar and salt to get an even coating of oil and spice. Place on the lined baking sheet and bake for 15 to 20 minutes—keep a close eye on it to avoid burning. Let cool and serve with the lemony cashew cream.

VE ✓

GF ✓

# Sweet Potato Chips

———

**Wholesome, but with a decadent feel, these colorful homemade chips with lemony cashew cream will be a favorite snack!**

———

SERVES 4

2 or 3 sweet potatoes, peeled

1 tablespoon olive oil

1 tablespoon apple cider vinegar

pinch of salt

ground cinnamon

TO SERVE

Lemony Cashew Cream (see left)

Preheat the oven to 300°F and line a baking sheet with parchment paper.

Put the sweet potato slices in a bowl and toss with the olive oil, apple cider vinegar, and salt. Place on the lined baking sheet and sprinkle with cinnamon. Bake for 20 minutes. It's important to keep an eye on them to decide if they are done—the chips should curl up and be fairly dry before their time. Let them cool and serve with lemony cashew cream.

VE ✓

GF ✓

# Onigiri

**Onigiri, Japanese rice balls, are often sold in Japanese delis and are a staple of the traditional Japanese bento lunch box. Even if you haven't yet tasted onigiri, you may well have seen the onigiri emojis, a sign of their rising popularity in the world. They are fun to make and can easily be varied with all kinds of flavorings and fillings, although I like to stick to typical Japanese ingredients—a mixture of furikake seasoning and pickles. The seasoning and fillings can either be mixed into the rice or used as a stuffing for the rice.**

SERVES 8

1½ cups Japanese or sushi rice (round, short-grained white rice)

1½ cups water

½ teaspoon salt

2 tablespoons black sesame seeds

5 by 2½-inch-long nori ribbons (cut from a sheet of nori)

PICKLES:

vegetables, such as carrot, beet, and cabbage or other greens

umeboshi or rice vinegar

salt, to taste

For the orange onigiri I used pickled carrots and umeboshi plums

For the green onigiri I used picked and massaged kale, scallions, fresh cilantro, and umeboshi plums

For the pink onigiri I used pickled radicchio, red onion, shiso leaf seasoning, and umeboshi plums

OTHER FLAVORING/FILLING OPTIONS:

crumbled smoked tofu mixed with wasabi-flavored mayonnaise

scallions, finely chopped

furikake (see page 166 for homemade)

nori

black sesame seeds

shiso leaf seasoning

To prepare the pickles, if you want to use them for flavoring/filling your onigiri, peel where appropriate and roughly chop the vegetables and/or shiso leaves, then put them in a ceramic or glass bowl. Pour over umeboshi or rice vinegar to cover and let stand at room temperature for 30 minutes. Massage the marinated vegetables for 2 minutes, then drain and chop very finely.

Put the rice in a sieve and rinse in several changes of cold water until the water is clear. Tip the drained rice into a saucepan that has a tight-fitting lid, stir in the measured water and salt, and bring to the boil. Reduce to a simmer, cover the pan with the lid, and cook for 20 minutes. Turn off the heat and leave the rice to steam, with the lid on, for about 10 minutes. Uncover and leave the rice to cool just slightly; it should still be warm when you form the onigiri.

You can now choose to stir together the cooked rice and the prepared pickled vegetables or herbs and/or microgreens or any other flavorings, such as umeboshi plums, smoked tofu and wasabi mayo, fresh herbs or scallions, or furikake. Any ingredient you want to mix into the rice needs to be chopped very finely. Alternatively, leave the rice as it is for stuffing once you have formed the onigiri.

Wet your hands and take a handful of rice. Gently press and mold the rice with your hands to form a triangular shape. If you want to stuff the onigiri, press your thumb into the rice to make a hollow in the center, add your chosen filling, and reshape the rice to enclose it. Sprinkle with the black sesame seeds or shiso leaf seasoning, if using, and wrap each onigiri with a nori strip.

The fillings can be prepared 2 days ahead and kept, tightly covered or in an airtight container, in the fridge. You can prepare the onigiri a day in advance and keep them, covered, in the fridge.

**VE** Opt for vegan mayonnaise; make your own furikake (see page 166) or look for fish-free furikake if buying ready-made.

**GF** Opt for gluten-free mayonnaise.

### Tip

*You will find shiso leaf seasoning in many well-stocked supermarkets or, if not, in Asian supermarkets or online, where you will also be able to source umeboshi vinegar. Japanese or sushi rice isn't a specific variety of rice but refers to a type of round, short-grained rice, which is slightly sticky when cooked.*

# Summary Rolls with Satay Dip

**MAKES 12**

12 round rice paper sheets, plus a few
    extra in case of casualties

SATAY PEANUT DIPPING SAUCE:

3 tablespoons good-quality smooth
    peanut butter
2 tablespoons shoyu soy sauce or tamari
1 tablespoon lime juice
1 teaspoon grated fresh ginger
1 garlic clove, crushed
1 teaspoon agave syrup or coconut sugar
¼ teaspoon sriracha sauce

SALAD FILLING:

2 medium carrots, peeled and julienned
    or cut into thin matchsticks
a handful of mixed salad leaves (I use
    spinach and radicchio), torn or shredded
2 handfuls of finely shredded red
    cabbage
1 red or yellow pepper, cored, seeded,
    and cut into strips
1 small Chioggia beet, peeled
    and sliced into thin half-moons
1 small cucumber, cut into thin
    matchsticks
1 medium avocado, thinly sliced
4 scallions, chopped
a handful of bean sprouts
a handful of cilantro

I remember when I took my first bite into a summer roll in a Vietnamese restaurant, and it was a revelation. I couldn't fathom how the taste could be so good when there was so little added flavoring apparent. I kept asking my food writer friend who had ordered the rolls for me if he was sure there wasn't a hidden ingredient somewhere. Soon after, I bought rice papers and made my own rolls at home, stunned that they proved so easy to prepare and could taste so amazing. With summer rolls, there is only one clear rule in my opinion—while the salad ingredients can be flexible, the key ingredient that gives them that characteristic heavenly light clean taste is the cilantro, so don't skip it! I just love this peanut sauce for dipping the rolls, but they are also delicious dipped into Japanese shoyu soy sauce (or tamari for a wheat-free alternative) or simply toasted sesame oil and rice vinegar. Sriracha sauce, a Thai hot chile sauce, is available from most Western supermarkets, Asian supermarkets, or online suppliers.

Mix together all the ingredients for the satay peanut dipping sauce in a bowl. This can be prepared a day before serving and kept, tightly covered or in an airtight container, in the fridge.

The rolls are best enjoyed freshly made, so prepare them just before guests arrive or let your guests make their own rolls.

Fill a bowl with lukewarm water. Dip a rice paper sheet in the water for 4 or 5 seconds. Transfer the rice paper to a work surface and wait a few seconds before adding the salad filling ingredients to the center of it. Carefully fold the sides of the rice paper, which should now be pliable, over the filling snugly, then fold the bottom and top edges in and roll up away from you, or leave the top edge open before rolling. Serve with the satay peanut dipping sauce.

**VE** ✓
**GF** Check the contents of the rice paper sheets
to ensure that they are gluten free; opt for
tamari sauce.

### Tip

*Want to make the rolls more substantial? Add 5 to 7 ounces thin rice noodles, rehydrated according to the package instructions and then rinsed in cold water and well drained, to the salad filling.*

# Butternut Squash Boats

SERVES 4

2 baby butternut squash, halved
    lengthwise and seeds and
    membrane removed
olive oil, for drizzling
a generous handful of torn stemmed
    cavolo nero (black kale) leaves
caramelized nuts, crushed
salt and freshly ground black pepper,
    to taste

PUMPKIN SEED AND DATE CREAM:

2 tablespoons pumpkin seed butter
    or other nut butter, such as almond
    butter or tahini
2 Medjool dates, pitted
2 tablespoons lemon juice
1 tablespoon orange blossom water
    (optional)
¼ teaspoon ground chile pepper
½ teaspoon salt
2 garlic cloves, crushed
3 tablespoons extra-virgin olive oil

**This is a delicious starter. The natural sweetness of the butternut squash is perfectly complemented by the nutty pumpkin seed and date cream, while the crispy cavolo nero and caremelized nuts add a lovely texture.**

Preheat the oven to 400°F. Line a large baking sheet with parchment paper. Arrange the butternut squash halves on the lined baking sheet, cut-side down, drizzle with olive oil, and season with salt and pepper. Bake for 30 minutes, then flip the halves over and bake for 10 minutes more, or until cooked through.

Combine the ingredients for the pumpkin seed and date cream in a food processor and process for a few seconds. Add small amounts of water until it reaches your desired consistency. Transfer to a bowl and cover until ready to serve. The cream can be prepared a day ahead and stored, covered, in the fridge.

Heat a skillet over medium-high heat. Drizzle in a small amount of olive oil, add the cavolo nero, and cook for about 1 minute, turning it over halfway through, just until crispy but not burnt. Sprinkle with salt to taste.

Transfer the butternut squash boats to a platter. Top with the crispy cavolo nero. Sprinkle with crushed caramelized nuts and drizzle with the pumpkin seed and date cream.

VE ✓
GF ✓

# Caramelized Onion Tarte Tatin

SERVES 8

SPELT PASTRY:
1⅓ cups spelt flour
¼ teaspoon salt
9 tablespoons butter, chilled, or coconut
    oil, soft but not liquid
about 2 tablespoons cold water

WHIPPED CHEESE:
7 ounces fresh goat's cheese
1½ teaspoons olive oil
sprinkle of salt

CARAMELIZED ONIONS:
5 tablespoons butter, or 3 tablespoons
    olive oil, for frying
1 pound red onions or a mix of red onions
    and shallots, halved, trimmed, and
    cut into wedges
2 teaspoons thyme leaves
2 tablespoons brown or coconut sugar
2 tablespoons red wine vinegar
salt, to taste

**This beautiful pie is a riff on the classic sweet tarte tatin, an upside-down pastry traditionally made with apples; here I'm using naturally sweet onions for a savory twist. Together with the salty crumbly pastry and whipped goat's cheese (or vegan soft cheese), this makes a great addition to a table of small dishes. But if you are making it as a starring dish, it's delicious served with a fresh salad. You can use ready-made pastry dough instead of making the spelt pastry.**

To make the pastry, mix together the flour and salt in a bowl. Add the butter or coconut oil in small pieces and rub it into the flour with your fingertips or work it in with a fork until evenly combined and the texture resembles breadcrumbs. Mix in the cold water to form a pliable mixture. Wrap in plastic wrap and let rest in the fridge for 30 minutes. The pastry can be made 2 to 3 days in advance and stored, wrapped, in the fridge.

Meanwhile, preheat the oven to 375°F. Put the ingredients for the whipped cheese in a bowl and whisk until fluffy. Cover and refrigerate until 15 minutes before serving.

Roll out the pastry between two sheets of parchment paper into a roughly square, ⅓-inch-thick sheet. Keep cool in the fridge until ready to use.

Heat a large ovenproof skillet (about 8 inches in diameter) over medium-high heat. Add the olive oil or butter, then arrange the onion wedges in a single snug layer in the pan. Season with salt and sprinkle with the thyme. Cover the pan with foil and bake for 35 minutes.

Remove from the oven, lift off the foil, and sprinkle the sugar and vinegar over the onions. Cut a round slightly larger than the pan from the pastry sheet. Lay the pastry round over the onions and tuck the edge in all round the inside of the pan to encase the onions. Bake for 20 to 25 minutes more, until the pastry is golden.

Remove the tart from the oven and let cool for a few minutes. Run a knife around the edge of the tart, then top the pan with a plate and, holding the plate firmly against the pan, invert the pan and plate together so that the tart transfers to the plate, with the pastry on the bottom. Serve hot or at room temperature with the whipped cheese.

**VE** Opt for vegan soft cheese and use olive oil for frying.
**GF** Use gluten-free pastry instead of the spelt pastry.

# Broccoli Soup and Feta Cream

SERVES 4

olive oil, for frying

2 shallots, finely diced

3 garlic cloves, crushed

2 tablespoons lemon juice

1 quart vegetable stock

2 medium potatoes, peeled and finely diced

1¼ pounds broccoli florets

a handful of fresh basil or mint

salt, to taste

pinch of freshly ground black pepper

FETA CREAM:

3½ ounces organic feta cheese, crumbled, or vegan yogurt mixed with 1 tablespoon nutritional yeast

6 tablespoons Greek or vegan yogurt

1 teaspoon honey or agave syrup

1 tablespoon extra-virgin olive oil

**This quick and easy soup has a good garlic hit balanced by tangy lemon, with the smooth and cooling feta and yogurt cream adding a contrasting highlight. Serve with freshly baked bread or salad.**

Put all the ingredients for the feta cream in a blender or food processor and blend until smooth. Set aside until ready to serve.

Heat a deep saucepan over medium heat. Add a drizzle of olive oil and fry the shallots for 5 to 6 minutes, stirring. Stir in all the remaining ingredients and bring to a boil, then reduce the heat and simmer for 10 minutes.

Transfer the soup to a blender or food processor and blend until smooth, or blend directly in the pan with an immersion blender. Serve topped with a drizzle of the feta cream.

Both the soup and the feta cream can be prepared 1 to 2 days in advance and kept, tightly covered or in an airtight container, in the fridge. Reheat the soup gently before serving.

VE Opt for vegan yogurt and nutritional yeast rather than feta cheese, vegan rather than Greek yogurt, and agave syrup instead of honey.

GF Opt for gluten-free tamari; serve with gluten-free bread or omit the bread.

# Zucchini Involtini

Serves 4 / Makes 12 rolls

1 pound ricotta or cottage cheese

2 garlic cloves, crushed

2 tablespoons lemon juice

½ teaspoon salt, or more to taste

¼ teaspoon freshly ground black pepper
   or a sprinkle of red pepper flakes

olive oil, for drizzling

about ¾ cup Marinara Sauce (see page
   143) or other tomato sauce

2 medium zucchini, each cut lengthwise
   into 6 thin slices (12 slices in total)

3½ ounces cavolo nero (black kale),
   stemmed, leaves leaves finely chopped

grated Parmesan, or rawmesan (see page
   28) or nutritional yeast for sprinkling

**Italian cooking is wonderful for allowing ingredients to shine in their own right. Here juicy zucchini rolls are filled with a zesty, garlicky cheese mixture and cavolo nero, and baked on a thin layer of classic Italian tomato sauce to deliver lots of satisfying flavor. Delizioso! The zucchini rolls also offer an ideal gluten-free alternative to pasta.**

**For a fresh herb take on this delicious dish, substitute basil or mixed tender summer herbs for the cavolo nero or add them, finely chopped, to the cheese mixture. To give the sugo sauce an extra dimension, blend in a roasted red pepper from a jar.**

Preheat the oven to 400°F. Mix together the cheese or vegan alternative, garlic, lemon juice, salt, and pepper or red pepper flakes in a bowl. Drizzle olive oil over the bottom of a large baking dish and pour in the tomato sauce.

To make the zucchini rolls, lay a zucchini slice on your work surface. Spread an even layer of the cheese mixture on top, then top with a thin layer of cavolo nero. Roll up and place in the sauce in the baking dish. Repeat with the remaining zucchini slices. Sprinkle the top with Parmesan, rawmesan, or nutritional yeast and bake for 20 to 25 minutes. Serve hot or at room temperature. You can prepare the rolls a day ahead and keep, tightly covered, in the fridge.

**VE** Opt for vegan soft cheese or crème fraîche
and rawmesan or nutritional yeast.
**GF** ✓

## Tip
*You can make this dish using thinly sliced eggplant in place of zucchini. Just add 5 to 10 minutes to the baking time.*

# Mini Caesar Salad Baskets

SERVES 8

9 ounces drained and rinsed canned
   chickpeas (optional)
2 avocados, chopped
8 large romaine lettuce leaves

VEGAN CAESAR DRESSING:
250ml vegan crème fraîche
2 tablespoons pine nuts
2 tablespoons nutritional yeast
2 tablespoons olive oil
1 tablespoon lemon juice
2 garlic cloves, peeled
1 teaspoon mustard
1 teaspoon drained capers
water, to thin the consistency

VEGETARIAN CAESAR DRESSING:
250ml crème fraîche
1 tablespoon pine nuts
2 tablespoons olive oil
1 tablespoon lemon juice
2 garlic cloves, peeled
1 teaspoon mustard
1 teaspoon drained capers

BASIC RAWMESAN:
2 tablespoons nutritional yeast
½ teaspoon salt
70g pine nuts or other nuts
   (walnuts are good)
1 garlic clove, minced

TOPPINGS:
grated Parmesan or rawmesan
   (see above)
pine nuts
capers
red onion, very thinly sliced
small croutons (I use sourdough) or
   panko breadcrumbs

**Here I've turned everyone's favorite salad into finger food! For this treat, use sturdy romaine lettuce leaves as edible bowls. My "sort of Caesar" dressing comes in both fully vegan and vegetarian versions, which are equally delicious. Add the chickpeas for a more filling starter.**

Put all the ingredients for the dressing of your choice in a blender and blend to your desired consistency. Transfer to a bowl, cover tightly, and refrigerate until ready to use. It will keep in the fridge for 3 to 4 days.

If using the chickpeas, heat a large skillet over medium-high heat, add the chickpeas, and cook, tossing frequently, for about 5 minutes until crispy. Tip the chickpeas onto a plate and let cool.

If you want to make rawmesan, mix the ingredients together in a food processor.

In a bowl, mix the avocado with the chickpeas, if using, and half the dressing. Fill the lettuce leaves with the avocado mixture, then top with the Parmesan or rawmesan, pine nuts, capers, red onion, and croutons or panko.

**VE** Use the vegan version of the Caesar dressing; opt for rawmesan for topping.
**GF** Use gluten-free croutons for topping.

# Curried Flatbread Pizza

MAKES 6 PIZZAS
6 flatbreads of your choice

CURRY PASTE:
ghee or vegetable oil, for frying
3 shallots, thinly sliced
1½ tablespoons red wine vinegar
    or lemon juice
2 garlic cloves, crushed
1 tablespoon grated fresh ginger
½ red chile, seeded and finely chopped
1½ teaspoons ground turmeric
1 teaspoon ground cinnamon
    or cardamom
1½ teaspoons ground cumin
1 teaspoon thyme leaves
½ teaspoon salt, or more to taste
¼ teaspoon freshly ground black pepper
a handful of almonds, coarsely ground
1 cup dairy or vegan yogurt
1 teaspoon honey or coconut sugar

SWEET GARLIC SAUCE:
½ cup plus 2 tablespoons Greek yogurt
1 garlic clove, minced
½ teaspoon honey or agave syrup
pinch of salt

TOPPING OPTIONS:
cherry tomatoes, sliced
fresh cilantro
baby spinach leaves
pickled red onion
piri piri peppers, finely chopped (for
    the hot spice lovers)
organic eggs

**When time is in short supply but I want to make something really delicious for friends and family, I often throw together these Indian-style pizzas, and they're always a hit! Don't be deterred by the list of ingredients, as the majority of them are spices you are likely to already have in your cabinets.**

**The idea is to use ready-made flatbreads (keep a stock of them in the fridge, as I do). I like to use thin Turkish flatbreads, but Indian naan bread or Italian piadina flatbreads work just as well. Simply spread them with curry paste and bake them like a pizza, then serve them with fresh toppings. This is homemade fast food at its best! The pizzas can also be served whole for a more substantial meal.**

Preheat the oven to 425°F. To make the curry paste, heat a skillet over medium-high heat. Add a generous spoonful of ghee or a good drizzle of vegetable oil and fry the shallots, stirring frequently, for about 2 minutes until transparent. Add the vinegar or lemon juice, garlic, spices, thyme, salt, and pepper and cook, stirring, for 2 to 3 minutes. Add the almonds and more ghee or vegetable oil, if needed, and fry, stirring frequently, for 1 to 2 minutes until the almonds are toasted. Reduce the heat, add the yogurt and the honey or coconut sugar, and cook, stirring constantly, for 2 to 3 minutes. Turn off the heat. The curry paste can be made 3 to 4 days in advance—let cool, transfer to an airtight container, and keep in the fridge.

Mix together the ingredients for the sweet garlic sauce in a small bowl and set aside until ready to serve.

Lay the flatbreads on a large baking sheet and spread with the curry paste. Bake for 30 seconds to 2 minutes, depending on the thickness of the breads, keeping an eye on them to avoid burning—if they are thin, they can quickly catch. I bake the breads in batches of 1 or 2 at a time. Remove from the oven, scatter with your choice of toppings, and drizzle with the garlic sauce. Cut into slices for sharing.

Tip
*Crack an egg over each flatbread before baking in the oven.*

VE Opt for vegetable oil and coconut sugar for the curry paste, and vegan yogurt and agave syrup for the sauce; don't use eggs as a topping.
GF Use gluten-free flatbreads, such as corn tortillas.

# Pink Grapefruit Margarita

A cocktail with lively citrus will open your get-together with zest! I use pink grapefruit for its beautiful color, but you can use any citrus you like. With its Mexican origins, this drink is a natural match for tacos and other Latin flavors.

SERVES 1
2½ tablespoons fresh pink grapefruit juice
2½ tablespoons tequila
1 tablespoon agave syrup
1 tablespoon fresh lime juice
ice cubes

SALTED HOT LIME RIM:
coarse sea salt
2 tablespoons water
1 tablespoon fresh lime juice
sprinkle of ground chile pepper

TO SERVE:
crushed ice
½ lime wheel

First prepare the salted hot lime rim. Make a layer of salt on a saucer or small plate. Mix together the water and lime juice in a shallow bowl. Dip the rim of a cocktail glass in the liquid to moisten it and then dip the rim in the salt to coat.

Put the pink grapefruit juice, tequila, agave syrup, and lime juice in a mixing glass with a few ice cubes and stir together well.

Add some crushed ice to a rimmed glass, then pour the cocktail through a sieve into the glass. Add the lime wheel half and serve.

Tip. *Simply omit the tequila for a zesty mocktail.*

VE ✓
GF ✓

# Mango Lassi

Refreshening and alcohol free, a smooth mango lassi will also chill the heat of a spicy curry, or cool you down on a hot summer's day. Lassi is a yogurt-based drink popular in India and surrounding countries and can be either savory or sweet. The most popular version of lassi worldwide is mango, which contains no added sugar, sweetened only by fresh mango pulp.

SERVES 2
1 ripe mango, chopped
grated zest of 1 lime
½ teaspoon fresh lime juice
2 cups yogurt, preferable coconut
pinch of ground cardamom (optional)
ice cubes

Put all the ingredients except the ice cubes in a blender and blend until smooth. Put some ice cubes in two glasses, pour over the mango lassi, and serve.

VE Opt for vegan yogurt.
GF ✓

Tip *Serve in cocktail glasses for a fruity mocktail.*

# Golden Milk Latte

Serving your guests this golden latte will make them feel extra nourished and cherished. Haldi ka doodh, or golden milk, as it's more often called in the Western world, is an Ayurvedic turmeric-flavored warm milk drink that has been enjoyed in India since ancient times. Golden milk is now making a splash outside of India, too, with a few tweaks to make it extra appealing to our Western palates. This version is sweetened with honey or agave syrup and has a touch of comforting cinnamon added.

SERVES 1
1 tablespoon finely grated fresh turmeric or ground turmeric
1 teaspoon honey or agave syrup
1 teaspoon finely grated fresh ginger
½ teaspoon fresh lemon juice
pinch of ground cardamom
pinch of ground cinnamon
pinch of freshly ground black pepper
1 cup dairy or plant-based milk of your choice

Put all the ingredients, except the milk, in a blender and blend to a smooth paste.

Bring the milk to a simmer in a saucepan, pour into the blender, and blend until combined. Serve in a glass or cup.

VE Opt for agave syrup and a plant-based milk.
GF ✓

# Rainbow Crudités with Artichoke Dip

Nothing shouts out "feast" more than a platter full to the brim with ripe vegetables in the colors of the rainbow! Choose quality ingredients and take care in cutting the vegetables into handy sizes and tempting shapes. The key to a successful veggie platter is to team up the crudités with a delicious savory dip.

The artichoke cream, made from the hearts of globe artichokes and flavored with mustard and capers, is just that, and this one is enhanced by fresh dill, plus a little yogurt for creamy perfection. The dip can be prepared a day ahead and the vegetables can be prepared on the same day and if covered well will keep fresh in the fridge for a few hours.

SERVES 6

2½ pounds fresh raw vegetables, such as cucumber, radishes, cauliflower, peppers, cherry tomatoes, carrots, and/or beets

ARTICHOKE DIP

10½ ounces jarred or canned artichoke hearts, drained
3 tablespoons crème fraîche
2 tablespoons finely chopped dill
1 garlic clove, crushed
1 teaspoon drained capers
3 tablespoons olive oil
1 tablespoon Dijon mustard
1 teaspoon honey or agave syrup
salt and freshly ground black pepper, to taste

Peel and trim the vegetables as necessary, then cut them into manageable and attractive sizes and shapes.

For the artichoke dip, combine the ingredients in a food processor and process to a smooth cream. To serve, arrange the vegetables and dip on a platter.

**VE** Opt for vegan crème fraîche and agave syrup instead of honey.
**GF** ✓

# Classic Hummus

Hummus is maybe one of the world's most popular dips. And for good reason: it's incredibly delicious! This recipe is based on classic hummus using a little yogurt for extra silky creaminess. You can vary the hummus by adding fresh herbs like cilantro, and veggies such as cooked squash or beets. Hummus can be prepared a day in advance and kept, tightly covered or in an airtight container, in the fridge. Serve with crudités or bread and swirl in some spicy harissa if you like a hot kick to it.

SERVES 4

2 garlic cloves, peeled
3 tablespoons water
2 (14-ounce) cans chickpeas, drained and rinsed
3 tablespoons tahini
2 tablespoons yogurt (optional)
1½ tablespoons lemon juice
salt, to taste
1 teaspoon harissa, for serving (optional)

In a blender, combine all the ingredients except the harissa and blend until smooth, adding small amounts of water until the hummus is at your desired consistency. Transfer to a bowl or shallow serving dish and swirl in the harissa, if desired.

**VE** Use vegan yogurt.
**GF** ✓

# Smoky Sweet Potato Tahini Pie

SERVES 4

SPELT PASTRY:

1⅓ cups spelt flour

¼ teaspoon salt

9 tablespoons butter, chilled, or coconut
     oil, soft but not liquid

about 2 tablespoons cold water

SWEET POTATO FILLING:

5 or 6 medium sweet potatoes

olive oil, for drizzling

1½ teaspoons dried thyme

3½ ounces Parmesan, finely grated

3½ ounces ricotta

2 tablespoons tahini

1½ teaspoons lemon juice

1 teaspoon honey or agave syrup

¾ tablespoon smoked paprika

a handful of caramelized almonds or
     pecans, to garnish

salt and freshly ground black pepper,
     to taste

**When you want a comforting meal to share, a savory pie is sure to delight everyone around the table. This pie features a simple spelt crust filled with creamy ricotta and sweet potato combined with tahini and smoked paprika, and topped with caramelized almonds, so there's plenty of flavor and texture at play here. Serve in slices, with a tangy green salad alongside.**

Preheat the oven to 425°F. Line a baking sheet with parchment paper.

To make the pastry, mix together the flour and salt in a bowl. Add the butter or coconut oil in small pieces and rub it into the flour with your fingertips or work it in with a fork until evenly combined and the texture resembles breadcrumbs. Mix in the cold water to form a dough. Wrap in plastic wrap and let rest in the fridge for 30 minutes. The pastry can be made 2 to 3 days in advance and stored, wrapped, in the fridge.

While the pastry is resting, start preparing the filling. Peel the sweet potatoes. Slice 10 thin rounds from one sweet potato and set them aside for the topping. Chop the remaining sweet potato into large dice (about ¾-inch pieces) and put in a bowl. Drizzle with olive oil and toss to coat evenly, then sprinkle with the thyme and season with salt and pepper. Spread out on the lined baking sheet and bake for 15 to 20 minutes, keeping watch on them to avoid burning. Remove from the oven and lower the oven temperature to 350°F.

Roll out the pastry and press it into a large (8- to 9-inch-diameter) pie dish to line the bottom and sides, then bake for 10 minutes. Meanwhile, put the roasted sweet potato in a food processor, add the remaining filling ingredients, and process to a smooth puree.

Tip the filling into the pie dish and arrange the reserved rounds of sweet potato on top. Bake for 30 minutes until browned on top. Sprinkle with the caramelized almonds and serve at room temperature.

The pie can be prepared a day ahead of serving and kept, covered, in the fridge.

**VE** Opt for coconut oil for the pastry; use rawmesan
(see page 28), vegan soft cheese, and agave syrup for
the filling.
**GF** Use gluten-free pastry instead of the spelt pastry.

# 2. MIDSUMMER FEAST

In Scandivania, around the time of the summer solstice, midsummer feasts are held throughout the day and long, light-filled nights. These feasts are often staged alfresco with the table adorned with freshly picked flowers, which guests also use to decorate their hair.

The food is a celebration of characteristic Nordic flavors, in particular fresh herbs and preserves, and a smörgåsbord—a wide variety of dishes—is the most popular form for the meal. But sometimes, all those flavors are gathered together in one dish, known as smörgåstårta—a savory sandwich cake.

Midsummer would not be complete without everyone enjoying a luscious strawberry sponge cake to round off the feast, before dancing barefoot and skinny-dipping late into the evening in a nearby lake or the sea. This chapter contains all the recipes you need to create your own Scandi-style summer feast.

# Green Pea and Broccoli Fritters

MAKES 12 FRITTERS

**DILL AND HORSERADISH CREAM:**
¾ cup Greek yogurt
2 tablespoons finely chopped dill
1 garlic clove, minced
1 tablespoon extra-virgin olive oil
1 teaspoon horseradish paste, or
   ½ teaspoon wasabi paste
½ teaspoon honey or agave syrup
½ teaspoon lemon juice
salt and freshly ground black pepper,
   to taste

**FRITTERS:**
7 ounces broccoli, chopped
3½ ounces grated Parmesan or
   rawmesan (see page 28)
7 ounces fresh or frozen peas
1 medium organic egg, lightly beaten
scant 1 cup panko breadcrumbs (optional)
½ teaspoon salt
¼ teaspoon freshly ground black pepper
vegetable oil, for frying

red onion, sliced or chopped, to serve
with the dill and horseradish cream

**Green peas and broccoli are bound together in these delicious Nordic-style falafels. Serve them as appetizers or as part of the smörgåsbord, or in a pita bread with salad as Scandinavian version of a falafel sandwich.**

**The contrastingly cool yogurt sauce is enhanced with horseradish and dill, flavorings that classically define Scandinavian cooking and are regarded as the Nordic equivalent of chile and garlic. You can substitute wasabi paste for the horseradish for an interesting twist.**

Mix together all the ingredients for the dill and horseradish cream in a bowl, then cover tightly and refrigerate until ready to serve. It can be made a day in advance and kept in the fridge.

Preheat the oven to 225°F. Line a baking sheet with parchment paper. Combine the fritter ingredients in a food processor and process until well mixed. Taste and adjust the seasoning with salt and pepper. Heat a skillet over medium-high heat. Add a drizzle of vegetable oil. Scoop up 1 tablespoon of the fritter mixture for each fritter and fry them, in batches, for 4 to 5 minutes, turning carefully to fry all sides. Transfer the fried fritters to the lined baking sheet and keep hot in the oven while you finish frying the remaining fritters.

Once all the fritters are fried, serve them with the dill and horseradish cream.

**VE** Opt for vegan yogurt, agave syrup, and rawmesan; omit the egg or use a vegan egg replacer.
**GF** Opt for gluten-free breadcrumbs.

# Smörgåsbord

SERVES 6

NEW POTATOES WITH DILL AND CHIVES:
2½ pounds new potatoes, lightly
scrubbed
pinch of salt, plus extra to taste
a handful of roughly chopped dill
1 tablespoon butter, or a drizzle of
olive oil
a handful of finely chopped chives

PICKLED VEGETABLES:
6 tablespoons apple cider vinegar
1 tablespoon sugar or agave syrup
1 teaspoon salt, plus a pinch
7 ounces prepped (peeled if appropriate
and thinly sliced or chopped) mixed
vegetables of your choice, such as
red onions, carrots, beet, cucumber,
zucchini, roasted cauliflower florets,
and cabbage

MUSTARD SOUR CREAM SAUCE:
½ cup plus 2 tablespoons sour cream or
vegan sour cream or crème fraîche
1 tablespoon Dijon mustard
1 teaspoon honey or agave syrup

Herbed Lentil Meatballs (see page 56)

OTHER SMÖRGÅSBORD ADDITIONS:
5 medium organic eggs, boiled for 8 to
10 minutes, drained, cooled in cold
water, and peeled
Smoked Tofu Rillette (see page 44)
red onion, finely chopped
knäckebröd (crispbreads) or crackers and
breads

**The Swedish smörgåsbord dates back to the sixteenth century and traditionally consists of a whole table of Scandinavian delicacies served cold and warm, and it remains today how Swedes enjoy holiday food. While all the dishes in this chapter are designed to work perfectly as part of a smörgåsbord, these are the all-important additions that complete the smörgåsbord experience. Pickles are always great for topping all sorts of savory food and Scandinavian pickles are no exception. These mixed pickled vegegetables in a creamy mustard sauce make the perfect vegetarian alternative to Swedish pickled herring—delicious served with boiled new potatoes with fresh herbs, hard-boiled eggs (or marinated tofu) and knäckebröd (Swedish crispbread) or other rustic bread like sourdough (as shown here) or rye bread.**

To prepare the potatoes, put them in a saucepan and cover generously with water. Add the salt and dill, bring to a boil, and cook until the potatoes are tender, 10 to 20 minutes, depending on the size of the potatoes. Drain the cooked potatoes and put them in a bowl. Add the butter or olive oil, sprinkle with salt to taste, and toss with the chives.

To prepare the pickled vegetables, mix together the vinegar, sugar or agave syrup, and salt in a large glass measuring cup. Pack the prepared vegetables into a sterilized large glass jar and pour over the pickling liquid. Seal the jar and set aside to pickle for 1 hour before serving. The pickled vegetables will keep in the sealed jar in the fridge for 10 to 14 days.

When ready to serve, mix together the sour cream, mustard, and a pinch of salt in a bowl. Drain the pickled vegetables and serve.

VE Opt for olive oil and vegan sour cream or
crème fraîche, butter, and cheese.
GF Use gluten-free crispbreads or crackers
and breads.

# Smoked Tofu Rillette

This sumptuous spread combining smoked tofu, garlic, and nutritional yeast brings a powerful, typically Scandinavian umami savor to breads, crackers, and Smörgåstårta (see page 47). Slightly smoky, almost fishy in flavor, with a rich creaminess, I use it as a faux mackerel spread on bread with pickles and fresh toppings. I've included a few optional variations in the ingredients, which are all equally delicious.

SERVES 4 TO 6/MAKES ABOUT 1 POUND
12 ounces smoked tofu
3½ ounces mayonnaise
2 tablespoons shoyu soy sauce or tamari
1 tablespoon nutritional yeast or grated Parmesan
1 garlic clove, minced
1 tablespoon extra-virgin olive oil
salt and freshly ground black pepper, to taste

OPTIONAL ADDITIONS/VARIATIONS
(CHOOSE ONE OR TWO):
2 tablespoons finely shredded ready-toasted nori
1 tablespoon finely chopped tarragon or dill
1 tablespoon finely chopped dragon fruit flesh
1 teaspoon lemon juice
1 tablespoon toasted sesame oil (substitute for the extra-virgin olive oil above)

Lightly press the smoked tofu between sheets of kitchen paper and leave for a few minutes to absorb the excess moisture.

Put all the ingredients in a blender or food processor and blend to a smooth cream. The rillette will keep in an airtight container in the fridge for 4 to 5 days.

**VE** Opt for vegan mayonnaise and nutritional yeast.
**GF** Opt for gluten-free tamari; opt for gluten-free mayonnaise.

# Green Garden Salad

This vibrant green salad combines lightly fried fresh asparagus and scallions with baby spinach, dressed with a zesty lemon and mustard dressing, to make the perfect side for Nordic dishes. Try substituting green beans or Broccolini for the asparagus to make this salad at other times of the year.

SERVES 4
a handful of medium asparagus spears
olive oil, for frying
4 scallions, thinly sliced
salt and freshly ground black pepper, to taste
a handful of baby spinach
9 ounces canned butter beans, drained and rinsed
4 medium organic eggs, boiled for 8 to 10 minutes, drained, cooled in cold water, and peeled
1 avocado, thinly sliced
1½ tablespoons capers

LEMON AND MUSTARD DRESSING:
1 tablespoon extra-virgin olive oil
1 tablespoon lemon juice
1½ teaspoons Dijon mustard
½ teaspoon honey or agave syrup

Whisk together the ingredients for the lemon and mustard dressing in a small bowl until well blended and set aside.

Snap or cut off the woody ends of the asparagus spears. Heat a wide skillet over medium-high heat. Add a drizzle of olive oil and fry the asparagus and scallions for about 3 minutes, turning frequently. Add the lemon juice and season to taste with salt and pepper.

Arrange the asparagus and scallions with the baby spinach and butter beans on a serving plate. Grate or crumble over the egg, or crumble over the tofu or sprinkle over the avocado. Sprinkle with the capers. Season lightly with salt and pepper and drizzle with the dressing.

**VE** Use 7 ounces crumbled smoked tofu instead of the eggs. Opt for agave syrup in the dressing.
**GF** ✓

### Seaweed caviar

*Seaweed caviar is the brilliant invention of modernist cuisine, an experimental and scientific style of cooking. By transforming liquefied seaweed into tiny pearls, the flavor and texture of caviar is achieved. Seaweed caviar is increasingly popular due to its delicious flavor, as caviar for vegetarians and vegans. As a food product, it is a far more eco-conscious choice than fish caviar. You will find it in fine food stores and online.*

# Smörgåstårta

SERVES 6

**LAYER 1:**
Smoked Tofu Rillette (see page 44)

**LAYER 2—NORDIC EGG SALAD:**
5 medium organic eggs, boiled for 8 to
    10 minutes, drained, cooled in cold
    water, and peeled
½ cup plus 2 tablespoons crème fraîche
5 tablespoons finely chopped chives
3 tablespoons finely chopped dill
1 tablespoon grated lemon zest
1 tablespoon Dijon mustard
salt and freshly ground black pepper,
    to taste

**LAYER 3—AVOCADO:**
mayonnaise, for spreading
4 avocados, thinly sliced (reserve a few
    slices to garnish)
squeeze of lemon juice

**TO ASSEMBLE:**
4 long slices of spelt or wheat bread, or
    gluten-free bread, crusts trimmed
½ cup plus 2 tablespoons mascarpone or
    crème fraîche

**TO DECORATE:**
a handful of fine sprouts, such as radish,
    alfalfa, or beet sprouts, and/or
    microgreens of your choice
½ red onion, pickled or finely chopped
2 or 3 radishes, thinly sliced
4 to 6 cucumber ribbons
2 tablespoons seaweed caviar (optional)

## Tip

*Ask your baker to slice the loaf of your
choice horizontally, then all you need to
do is trim the crusts. You can also piece
together squares of presliced sandwich
bread—just trim the crusts and make sure
the slices are the same size.*

**This over-the-top sandwich cake holds the number one spot in
Sweden for party food at milestone celebrations, such as birthdays
and graduation parties. With the rising interest in Nordic food culture,
smörgåstårta has gained an elevated status in recent times and you can
now often find versions of this once folksy cake in refined restaurants.
Traditionally made with shrimp, salmon, or ham, my version replicates
all the characteristic flavors of the original using my delicious Smoked
Tofu Rillette (see page 44), egg salad, and avocado. The ingredients
for decorating the cake can be varied according to the season, or make
your own creative choices. Make the cake entirely vegan by substituting
Artichoke Dip (see page 34) or your bean dip of choice for the egg salad.**

Mix together all the ingredients for the Nordic egg salad in a bowl. You can
prepare this a day ahead and store it, tightly covered, in the fridge.

To assemble the cake, lay a sheet of parchment paper on a tray or wooden
board. Place a slice of bread on the paper and spread with an even layer of
the smoked tofu rillette. Top with another slice of bread. Spread the second
layer with an even layer of the egg salad. Add a third slice of bread and spread
with a thin layer of mayonnaise, then arrange the avocado slices on top in an
even layer and squeeze over a little lemon juice. Add the fourth slice of bread.
Spread the mascarpone or crème fraîche over the top and sides of the cake.
Decorate with the ingredients listed and serve as soon as possible.

**VE** Opt for vegan crème fraîche and mayonnaise. Use
Artichoke Dip (see page 34) or vegan bean spread or
dip in place of the egg salad.
**GF** Use gluten-free bread and mayonnaise.

Tip

To achieve the appropriate flavor without using Västerbotten cheese, use a 50:50 mixture of aged mature Cheddar and Parmesan.

# Västerbotten Pies

SERVES 6

1 recipe Spelt Pastry (see page 22)
10½ ounces prepared vegetables, such as broccoli or spinach, tomatoes, potatoes, or leeks

FILLING:

9 ounces Västerbotten cheese or other sharp nutty dairy cheese (see Tip), or vegan hard cheese, grated
3 medium organic eggs
6 tablespoons half-and-half or full-fat Greek yogurt
6 tablespoons dairy or plant-based milk of your choice
3 bird's-eye chiles, seeded, except for a few seeds, and pounded to a paste using a mortar and pestle (optional)
pinch of salt and pinch of freshly ground black pepper

TOPPINGS

red onion
yogurt
tomatoes

The indulgent, rich, and creamy filling of these pies is made with Västerbotten cheese, an aged Swedish cheese with a pronounced flavor reminiscent of a mixture of Parmesan and Cheddar. Here I've taken the traditional recipe further by adding vegetables to the filling because, as we all know, cheese and veggies are a match made in heaven. I've also added a bit of heat to the pies, using sharp piri piri, inspired by my artist friend Adelaster, who served a chile-hot version of Västerbotten pie when I visited her in Sweden. Traditionally, this pie uses dairy cheese and cream, but the filling can easily be made with plant-based ingredients— try using blended silken tofu or dairy-free cream, or cashew cream, instead of cheese and half-and-half, and add vegan cheese or 2½ ounces nutritional yeast and adjust the taste with salt, pepper, and olive oil.

———

Preheat the oven to 425°F. Prepare the vegetables by boiling scrubbed or peeled potatoes for up to 20 minutes or until soft in the middle. Drain and slice thinly. If using a whole broccoli, cut into florets and steam for 4 minutes before cutting into smaller pieces. If using leeks, cut them into thin slices.

Press the pastry into six 2½- to 2¾-inch-diameter tartlet tins or one large (10-inch-diameter) flan/quiche pan to line the bottom and sides, then bake for 10 minutes. Meanwhile, put all the ingredients for the filling in a blender or food processor and blend until smooth.

Pour the filling into the tartlet tins or flan pan and add the prepared vegetables, distributing them evenly. Bake for 12 to 15 minutes for the small pies and 20 minutes for the large pie. Let cool before serving.

The cooked pies can be baked up to 2 days before serving and stored, covered, in the fridge.

VE Opt for coconut oil in the pastry; use vegan cheese, vegan yogurt, vegan egg replacer, vegan cream, and plant-based milk for the filling.
GF Use gluten-free pastry.

# Midsummer Dream Cake

SERVES 8

### SPONGE CAKE

2 cups spelt flour

¾ cup raw cacao powder or cocoa
   powder

2 teaspoons baking powder

⅔ teaspoon fine salt

½ teaspoon ground cardamom

½ cup plus 1 tablespoon coconut oil or
   butter, plus extra for greasing

1 ripe banana, mashed to a smooth puree

½ cup plus 3 tablespoons plant-based or
   dairy milk

grated zest of ½ orange

3 tablespoons mango or fresh orange
   juice

2 teaspoons vanilla extract

125g honey or agave syrup

### RASPBERRY FILLING:

7 ounces mascarpone or crème fraîche

1 teaspoon fresh lemon juice

2½ ounces raspberries, fresh or frozen

2 tablespoons honey or agave syrup

### MASCARPONE FROSTING:

7 ounces mascarpone or crème fraîche

3 tablespoons honey or agave syrup

1 teaspoon fresh lemon juice

½ teaspoon vanilla extract

pinch of salt

ground cinnamon, for dusting

### DECORATION

10½ ounces strawberries, halved

other berries and fresh wild flowers
   (optional)

Most Swedes would agree that midsummer wouldn't be the same without a proper strawberry sponge cake. Swedish sponge cakes are often made extra juicy by the addition of fruit juice, and in this case I've chosen to use mango and orange juice, along with a touch of cardamom for extra aromatic interest. I wanted to devise a sponge cake recipe without using eggs, so I've added mashed banana instead. That and the use of spelt flour, which I really like in baking for its nutty flavor, makes the sponge a little denser and moister than the traditional kind. It's also easy to substitute plant-based ingredients for the dairy items in the filling and frosting as suggested.

To decorate, use a few common edible wild flowers if you have the opportunity to pick them—after all, midsummer is all about celebrating the great outdoors in full bloom!

—

Preheat the oven to 350°F and grease an 8-inch springform pan with coconut oil. Put the dry ingredients in a large bowl and whisk well. Melt the coconut oil or butter slowly in a pan. Put the honey, milk, orange zest, juice, mashed banana and vanilla extract in a second bowl and add the melted oil or butter. Whisk the wet ingredients together, either by hand or using a handheld mixer.

Pour the wet mixture into the bowl with the dry ingredients and mix well. Pour the batter into the greased pan and level the top with a spatula or the back of a spoon. Bake for 1 hour. Test by inserting a skewer into the center: if it comes out dry and clean, the cake is cooked. Bake for a few minutes longer if it needs it. Remove from the oven and allow the cake to rest and cool.

To make the raspberry filling, mix all the ingredients together. Set aside in the fridge. To make the mascarpone frosting, briskly whip all the frosting ingredients together in a large bowl. Refrigerate until ready to assemble the cake.

When the cake is cool, halve it horizontally; gently lift off the top half and set aside carefully. Add a generous layer of raspberry filling to the bottom cake layer, then place the top half over the filling. Carefully spread a thick, even layer of the mascarpone frosting over the top of the cake.

Decorate the assembled cake with halved strawberries. It looks beautiful and festive to arrange flowers and berries around the bottom or on top with the strawberries.

**VE** Use coconut oil or olive oil instead of butter; opt for agave syrup instead of honey; and use vegan crème fraîche instead of mascarpone and cottage cheese.

**GF** This cake is not gluten-free.

# 3. MIDWINTER FEAST

A variety of comforting dishes is what's needed to create a warm, welcoming Midwinter table, and in this chapter, colorful beets and greens are used to create a feast for the eye as well as the taste buds. But it wouldn't be complete without a centerpiece roast, so here you'll also find a whole thyme and garlic-roasted cauliflower and mustard-and-miso-rubbed celeriac served sliced into steaks. To contrast and complement, there are fresh, sweet and tangy sides featuring cabbage, onion and citrus, and roots roasts, while a delicious gravy adds a luxurious enriching element to that Swedish essential—meatballs—here reinterpreted with lentils and herbs—and root roasts. And for a show-stopping finish, there is an impressive chocolate cake with deep, dark flavors from dates and beet. Winter never tasted so good!

# Warm Mulled Apple Juice

Mulled warm drinks, especially spiced wines, are essential during the festive winter season in northern Europe. This alchol-free mulled apple juice is both refreshing and warming, the spices add a beautiful flavor and best of all it can be shared with everyone, from children to designated drivers.

MAKES 2 QUARTS

2 quarts good-quality unsweetened apple juice
2 tablespoons honey or agave syrup
5 cloves
2 cinnamon sticks, plus extra to serve
4 star anisepods, plus extra to serve
slices of citrus fruit, plus extra to serve

Put all the ingredients, except the extras for serving, in a large saucepan that has a lid. Bring to a boil, then reduce the heat, cover the pan with the lid, and simmer for 30 minutes.

To serve, ladle into cups or handled glasses and add an extra star anisepod , a citrus slice, and a cinnamon stick to each.

**VE** Opt for agave syrup.
**GF** ✓

# Blackberry Onion Confit

The natural sweetness of the red onions is intensified in this jam-like condiment, which acts well as a counterbalance to intensely savory dishes. It's delicious served with root vegetables. The optional puréed blackberries can be swapped out for other berries or fruit, such as cranberries, blueberries, cloudberries, and/or figs.

MAKES ABOUT 10½ OUNCES

olive oil or unsalted butter, for frying
3 medium red onions, thinly sliced
¼ cup coconut sugar or agave syrup
¼ cup red wine vinegar
2 tablespoons pureed blackberries (optional)
pinch of salt

Heat a skillet over medium heat. Add a drizzle of olive oil or a little butter and fry the onions for 10 to 12 minutes, stirring, until soft and just translucent. Add the remaining ingredients and cook over low heat, stirring, for 10 minutes until the liquid has reduced. Transfer to a sterilized jar, seal, and let cool.

The confit can be stored in the fridge for up to 5 days. Let sit at room temperature for 1 hour before serving.

**VE** Opt for olive oil.
**GF** ✓

# Herbed Lentil Meatballs with Green Peppercorn Gravy

SERVES 6/MAKES 32 MEATBALLS

HERBED LENTIL MEATBALLS:

5 cups cooked Puy or green lentils
¼ cup finely chopped thyme leaves
5 ounces onion, finely chopped and sautéed
2 cups panko breadcrumbs or cooked brown rice
4 garlic cloves, crushed
¼ cup nutritional yeast or grated Parmesan
2 teaspoons salt, plus extra to taste
½ teaspoon freshly ground black pepper, plus extra to taste
1 tablespoon mustard
2 generous handfuls of delicate herbs, such as basil and flat-leaf parsley, finely chopped
1 teaspoon honey or agave syrup
olive oil or ghee or butter, for frying

GREEN PEPPERCORN GRAVY:

2 tablespoons ghee or butter or vegetable oil
2 tablespoons drained green peppercorns in brine
2 tablespoons apple puree
½ cup plus 2 tablespoons vegetable stock
3 tablespoons soy or tamari sauce
½ cup plus 2 tablespoons heavy cream
salt, to taste
1 tablespoon kuzu or rice flour or all-purpose flour, for thickening (optional)

As with the Midsummer Feast (see page 39), the Swedish Christmas table is a smörgåsbord of savory dishes, along with pickles and slightly sweet sides, and typically Swedish meatballs. Here I've adapted my "neatballs" recipe from *Bowls of Goodness*, using cooked lentils and fresh fragrant herbs, perfectly complemented by a piquant green peppercorn gravy, making a delicous Midwinter Feast dish. Serve with the Blackberry Onion Confit (see page 55) and Gratin Dauphinois (see page 58), puffed potatoes (see page 65), or mashed potatoes.

To prepare the meatballs, mix together all the ingredients in a bowl, then transfer to a food processor and pulse for a few seconds until coarsely ground—be careful not to overprocess or the mixture will become too smooth. Return the mixture to the bowl, cover, and let rest in the fridge for 30 minutes.

Preheat the oven to 225°F. Line a baking sheet with parchment paper. Wet your hands, or oil them, and form the mixture into small balls about 1 inch in diameter. Heat a skillet over medium-high heat. Add a drizzle of olive oil or a little ghee or butter and fry the balls, in batches, for 2 to 3 minutes. Transfer the fried balls to the lined baking sheet and keep warm in the oven while you finish frying all the balls or until ready to serve.

Meanwhile, to make the green peppercorn gravy, heat a saucepan over medium-high heat. Add the ghee, butter, or vegetable oil; once hot, add all the remaining ingredients except the thickener and whisk the gravy until it's smooth and hot. Taste and adjust the seasoning with salt. If you want to thicken the gravy, crush the kuzu using a mortar and pestle, then dissolve it in 2 tablespoons of cold water, add to the sauce, and whisk until combined and smooth. If you are using rice flour or all-purpose flour, mix with 1 tablespoon cold water to a smooth paste, then whisk into the gravy. Simmer for a couple of minutes until thickened. Serve the warm herbed lentil meatballs with the green peppercorn gravy.

## Tip
*Add 1 tablespoon Cognac to the sauce for extra flavor, unless serving to children.*

VE Opt for olive oil for frying; nutritional yeast and agave syrup for the meatballs; and vegetable oil and vegan cooking cream for the gravy.
GF Opt for cooked brown rice or use gluten-free breadcrumbs instead of panko for the meatballs; use gluten-free tamari for the gravy.

# Gratin Dauphinois with Roasted Leeks

**Gratin Dauphinois will have great sentimental value for those who, like me, grew up in the seventies and eighties, as it was the go-to festive potato dish. For everyone else, it's just an incredibly tasty, classic French dish. Covering thin slices of potato in a garlicy creamy sauce is just brilliant, and it works decade after decade! This decadent gratin can be custom-made to suit everyone: read the note on cream and milk below.**

SERVES 6

2¼ pounds waxy potatoes, scrubbed, and thinly sliced on a mandoline or with a knife

2 garlic cloves, minced

2 shallots, thinly sliced

1 cup cream of choice, see note

1 cup plant-based or dairy milk

1¼ teaspoons salt

½ teaspoon freshly ground black pepper

2 teaspoons thyme leaves, plus extra for sprinkling

2 small baby leeks or 4 scallions, ends trimmed off and halved lengthways

3½ ounces rawmesan (see page 28) or Parmesan or other cheese of choice, grated

a drizzle of olive oil

Preheat the oven to 325°F. Grease a large baking dish and arrange the potato slices in the dish in overlapping layers. Combine the garlic, shallots, cream, milk, salt, pepper, and thyme in a saucepan. Bring to a boil, then reduce the heat to simmer. Stir and simmer for 5 minutes. Pour over the potatoes.

Brush the leeks with olive oil and press them down into the gratin. Bake for 50 to 60 minutes, keeping an eye on them in the last 10 minutes to avoid burning. Sprinkle with cheese and bake for an additional 10 minutes. Serve warm with other dishes such as the lentil meatballs (see page 56) or roasted cauliflower (see page 61).

**VE** Opt for plant-based milk, vegan cream, and rawmesan (see page 28).

**GF** ✓

### Cream of the crop!

*Many classic French dishes and "old-school" cooking in general can be heavy on dairy cream, butter, and cheese, but if you are looking to decrease your intake of animal protein, there are many good options for replacing dairy.*

*The good news is that you can enjoy it all, with some tweaks; wherever a recipe calls for butter, use olive oil instead. Natural food stores are stocking more plant-based creams as the vegan diet is becoming increasingly popular. Diluted nut butters and coconut milk, cashew cream, and silken tofu all make good alternatives to dairy cream.*

# Cauliflower Roast

**Cauliflower is a champion in the kitchen, making delicious roasts as well as mashes and sauces. This roast uses a simple rub of garlicky olive oil, finished with nutritional yeast or Parmesan and lemon juice, allowing the natural flavor of the cauliflower to shine.**

SERVES 6 (AS A SIDE)

6 tablespoons olive oil, plus extra if needed
2 garlic cloves, crushed
1 large cauliflower, about 2¼ pounds, leaves removed and stalk trimmed
4 or 5 thyme sprigs
1½ ounces nutritional yeast or Parmesan, grated
juice of 1 lemon
1 tablespoon agave syrup
salt and freshly ground black pepper, to taste

CASHEW TAHINI SAUCE:

1 tablespoon tahini
1 tablespoon shoyu soy or tamari
⅔ cup pre-soaked cashew nuts, drained
1 tablespoon olive oil
1½ tablespoons lemon juice
1 garlic clove, crushed
1 teaspoon agave syrup or honey
½ teaspoon salt and more, to taste
water, to thin

Preheat the oven to 425°F. Mix together half the olive oil and all the garlic in a small bowl. Drizzle some over the cauliflower on a baking sheet. Turn the cauliflower upside down and lightly drizzle or spray the inside with the rest of the garlicky olive oil. Insert thyme sprigs into the spaces between the florets, then sprinkle with salt and pepper. Roast for 1 hour.

When the cauliflower is roasting, blend the cashew tahini sauce together until smooth. Add small amounts of water until desired consistency.

Remove the cauliflower from the oven and let cool slightly. Meanwhile, mix the remainder of the olive oil with the nutritional yeast or Parmesan, lemon juice, and agave syrup in a small bowl. Drizzle over and then rub into the roasted cauliflower. Roast for an additional 5 minutes. Transfer the whole cauliflower to a serving platter, then slice to serve.

**VE** Opt for nutritional yeast.
**GF** ✓

*You can easily vary the seasoning rub for the cauliflower by using tikka masala or harissa and tahini blended with olive oil and salt or vegetarian or vegan pesto.*

# Winter Coleslaw

**In the winter, cabbage often replaces more tender green leaves in my salads. This vibrant coleslaw adds a fresh contrast to fried and roasted dishes.**

SERVES 6

½ head green cabbage, finely shredded
½ head red cabbage, finely shredded
½ red onion, thinly sliced
2 carrots, julienned
a small handful of fresh mint, parsley or coriander, thinly sliced
½ cup walnuts, crumbled

MUSTARD MAYONNAISE

1 tablespoon Dijon mustard
1 teaspoon apple cider vinegar
3 tablespoons mayonnaise or vegan mayonnaise
juice of ½ lemon (about 1 tablespoon)
½ teaspoon salt, plus extra to taste
1 teaspoon olive oil

Mix the first six ingredients together in a small bowl. Toss the remaining ingredients in a serving bowl. Pour the mustard-mayo mixture over and toss to combine.

**VE** Opt for vegan mayonnaise.
**GF** Opt for gluten-free mayonnaise.

*From top left:*
*Chai Carrot Cake, page 186. Mini Caesar Salad Baskets, page 28. Lemon Butternut Soup, page 139. Seared Brussels Sprouts with Pomegranate Seeds, page 64. Best Tomato Salad Ever (with spinach and avocado and sourdough croutons added), page 138. Roasted Baby Pumpkins Stuffed with Harissa Lentils, page 115. Cauliflower Roast, page 61. Winter Coleslaw, page 61.*
*Green Pancakes, from the Green Crêpe Cake, page 154.*

# Citrus Salad

A zingy citrus salad brightens up winter dinners and delivers a dose of vitamin D as a bonus. And it doesn't need much to shine—a simple vinaigrette and fresh herbs will do the trick. Include the spinach and nuts to make a more substantial side dish or just serve the fruits dressed with the vinaigrette and herbs for a pure citrus experience.

SERVES 4 (AS A SIDE)
6 oranges or blood oranges
4 clementines
1 grapefruit
fresh mint and basil, roughly chopped
baby spinach leaves, to serve (optional)
toasted walnuts, to serve (optional)

VINAIGRETTE:
3 tablespoons olive oil
2 tablespoons red vinegar
1 teaspoon honey or agave syrup
½ teaspoon salt

Whisk together all the ingredients for the vinaigrette in a small bowl until well blended.

To prepare the citrus fruits, take each fruit in turn and slice off the top and bottom, just deep enough to expose the flesh. Sit the fruit firmly on your cutting board and slice downward, following the curve of the fruit, to cut away the peel, white pith, and thin membrane on the outside of the fruit sections, turning the fruit as you continue to work around it. Then slice each fruit crosswise into rounds ¼ inch thick.

Arrange the fruit rounds on a serving plate, drizzle with the vinaigrette, and sprinkle with the herbs. Serve with spinach and walnuts, if you like.

VE Opt for agave syrup.
GF ✓

# Seared Brussels Sprouts with Pomegranate

Strikingly emerald green and ruby in color, this dish is certain to add festive flair to any table. The earthy brassica taste of Brussels sprouts marries particularly well with the tart sweetness of pomegranate, and frying the sprouts in ghee or butter (or olive oil for a vegan alternative) with garlic gives a boost to their flavor.

SERVES 6 AS A SIDE
2 tablespoons lemon juice
1 teaspoon honey or agave syrup
2 tablespoons pomegranate juice
ghee, butter or olive oil, for frying
2 garlic cloves, crushed
1¾ pounds Brussel sprouts, trimmed and halved
3½ ounces pomegranate seeds
salt and freshly ground black pepper, to taste

Mix together the lemon juice, honey or agave syrup, and pomegranate juice in a small bowl and set aside.

Heat a skillet over medium-high heat. Add a generous amount of ghee, butter, or olive oil and the garlic and fry the sprouts, cut-side down, for 2 minutes without disturbing. Flip the sprouts over, season with salt and pepper, and drizzle with the lemon juice mixture, then fry for an additional 5 minutes, ensuring that they cook evenly on their rounded side.

Transfer to a serving dish and sprinkle with the pomegranate seeds.

VE Opt for agave syrup and olive oil.
GF ✓

# Endive and Pear Gratin

Endive gratins are hugely popular in the Netherlands, Belgium, and northern France. My version is topped with slices of sweet pear and pine nuts. You can adjust the cream and cheese to your preference.

SERVES 6

olive oil, for greasing and drizzling
5 endives, halved
1 small firm pear, cored and sliced
3 garlic cloves, minced
1 cup cream of your choice
6 tablespoons plant-based or dairy milk
¾ teaspoon salt, plus extra to taste
¼ teaspoon freshly ground black pepper
3½ ounces Parmesan, finely grated or
    rawmesan (see page 28)
thyme sprigs
a handful of pine nuts

Preheat the oven to 425°F. Grease a baking dish and arrange the endive halves in the dish snugly in a single layer. Add the pear slices.

Combine the garlic, cream, milk, salt, pepper, and thyme in a saucepan. Bring to a boil, then reduce the heat to simmer. Stir and let simmer for 2 minutes. Pour over the endives and pear. Press the endive and pear down into the gratin so everything is covered with the cream and bake for 25 minutes.

Sprinkle with cheese, add a few thyme sprigs and pine nuts, and bake for an additional 10 minutes. Serve warm. Drizzle with olive oil and salt lightly before serving

VE Use vegan cream and cheese and plant-based milk.
GF ✓

# Puffed Potatoes

These potatoes are roasted long enough to develop a puffed appearance, which gives them an extra delicious taste. Serve them as a side or with lentil meatballs (see page 56).

SERVES 6

1 pound waxy potatoes, cut into thick wedges
olive oil
salt
1 tablespoon thyme leaves

Preheat the oven to 425°F. Put the potato wedges in a baking dish, toss with the olive oil, salt, and thyme, and roast for 40 to 45 minutes.

VE ✓
GF ✓

# Beet Ravioli with Winter Pesto Sauce

**Beet filling:**
2 large beets, washed and peeled
3½ ounces Parmesan, grated, or
    rawmesan (see page 28)
⅔ cup panko breadcrumbs

**Fresh pasta dough:**
1½ cups all-purpose flour
¾ cup plus 2 tablespoons semolina flour,
    plus extra for dusting
large pinch of salt
4 medium organic eggs, lightly beaten

**Winter pesto sauce:**
2 handfuls of winter green leaves (stalks
    removed), such as kale, cavolo nero
    (black kale) or spinach
juice of 1 lemon
2 garlic cloves, crushed
1¾ ounces Parmesan, grated
5 tablespoons extra-virgin olive oil
a handful of pistachio nuts or pine nuts
3 tablespoons mascarpone or crème
    fraîche
salt, to taste

**To finish:**
pinch of salt
olive oil
a few drops of truffle oil (optional)

**Embrace the season's hearty flavors by serving up beautiful plates of beet ravioli with a pesto sauce made from winter greens. Roasting the beets mellows their earthiness and brings out their sweetness. Serve as a main dish or a side.**

Put the beets in a food processor with the Parmesan or rawmesan and panko breadcrumbs and process to a grainy paste. Remove from the food processor and set aside.

Make the pasta dough. Mix together the flours and salt in a large bowl. Make a well in the center, add the eggs to the well, and, using your hands, gradually mix the egg with the flour into a dough. Knead the dough on a work surface for 3 to 4 minutes until smooth. Wrap the dough in plastic wrap and let rest at room temperature for 30 minutes.

Meanwhile, make the pesto sauce. Put the greens in a bowl, sprinkle with the lemon juice, and massage with your hands for a couple of minutes until the leaves have softened. Transfer to a food processor, add the remaining pesto ingredients, and process until smooth. Transfer to a saucepan and set aside.

To make the ravioli, dust some clean dish towels and a work surface generously with semolina flour. Divide the pasta dough into quarters and keep those you aren't working with covered with plastic wrap. Take one quarter and roll it out on the prepared work surface into an even thin sheet about 2mm thick. Working quickly, cut the sheet into rounds using a 2¾-inch round cookie or biscuit cutter. Add 1 teaspoon of the filling to the center of each round, then brush the edges with water, fold one side over the filling to make a half-moon, and press the edges together lightly to seal. Once sealed, immediately transfer the ravioli to a floured dish towel. Repeat with the remaining dough and filling.

Bring a large saucepan filled with water to a boil. Meanwhile, heat a large skillet over low heat and add a drizzle of olive oil. Add a pinch of salt and a drizzle of olive oil to the boiling water and cook the ravioli, in batches, for 2 minutes. Remove the cooked ravioli with a slotted spoon and transfer to the skillet to keep warm until all the ravioli are cooked.

While the ravioli are cooking, heat the pesto sauce over low heat and simmer for 2 minutes. Serve the ravioli with the pesto sauce and a few drops of truffle oil, if using.

**VE** Use vegan wonton wrappers instead of pasta dough, and opt for rawmesan (see page 28) and vegan crème fraîche.
**GF** Use gluten-free dried breadcrumbs instead of panko, and gluten-free wonton wrappers instead of pasta dough.

**Tip**
*Using wonton wrappers instead of making the pasta is a handy shortcut if you're running out of time.*

*You can replace the kuzu with another thickening agent, such as arrowroot, or add vegan cooking cream or heavy cream for extra creaminess.*

# Hasselback Celeriac Steak with Mushroom and Shallot Gravy

SERVES 6

1 celeriac (celery root), about 1¾ pounds

HERB AND MUSTARD RUB:

¾ cup plus 2 tablespoons panko
    breadcrumbs

3 tablespoons almond butter

2 tablespoons thyme leaves

1 tablespoon rosemary leaves

1 tablespoon lemon juice

3 garlic cloves, crushed

¾ teaspoon salt

3 tablespoons olive oil

1 tablespoon mustard

1 tablespoon red miso paste or brown
    rice miso paste (genmai)

MUSHROOM AND SHALLOT GRAVY:

1 tablespoon kuzu (optional)

2 tablespoons cold water (if using kuzu)

2½ tablespoons butter, or 2 tablespoons
    olive oil

2½ ounces mixed mushrooms, such as
    shiitake and oyster, finely chopped

2 shallots, finely chopped

1 tablespoon chopped tarragon

3 tablespoons dry sherry or sake, or
    other sweet wine

1 cup vegetable stock

**Hasselback potatoes has been popular in Sweden since the 1950s when it was first served in Hasselbacken, as restaurant in Sweden. The hasselback technique means cutting scores through potatoes, adding extra texture to the bite, and it can be used on a variety of root vegetables and squashes. Celeriac (celery root) may have a unflattering rough exterior, but it makes an impressive roast, as the flesh within has a lot of character—more than most other roots, in fact—with an earthy yet clean and sharp celery-like flavor that is mellowed and sweetened with roasting. I serve it with a creamy mushroom and shallot gravy for a balance of texture and bite.**

Put all the ingredients for the herb and mustard rub in a blender or food processor and process until well combined. Set aside.

Preheat the oven to 375°F. Trim the sprouty roots from the celeriac and scrub it clean. Set the celeriac on a sheet of foil. Using a sharp knife, cut the celeriac into thin slices down from the top to about three-quarters of the way through the celeriac, leaving the last quarter at the bottom uncut. Brush the celeriac generously with the rub, working it down inside the cuts as deep as you can go. Wrap in the foil, set on a baking sheet, and roast for 2 to 2½ hours, until the celeriac is cooked through, opening up the foil wrapping for the last 30 minutes of roasting.

Meanwhile, make the mushroom and shallot gravy. If you want to thicken the gravy, crush the kuzu using a mortar and pestle, then dissolve it in the cold water and set aside. Heat a skillet over medium-high heat. Add the butter or olive oil and fry the mushrooms and shallots with the tarragon for 7 to 8 minutes, stirring frequently. Stir in the sherry, sake, or wine and the stock, reduce the heat to low, and simmer for 4 to 5 minutes. Add the kuzu mixture, if using, and whisk until combined and smooth. Simmer for a couple of minutes until thickened. Set aside and reheat before serving.

To serve, drizzle a few tablespoons of the reheated mushroom and shallot gravy on a serving platter and add the roasted celeriac. Serve the celeriac in slices, drizzled with the gravy.

**VE** Opt for olive oil.
**GF** Use gluten-free dried breadcrumbs
instead of panko.

# Date and Beet Chocolate Cake with Lingonberry Glaze

2 or 3 beets (about 7 ounces), peeled and chopped

8 dried Medjool dates, soaked in water for 30 minutes to 2 hours, then drained and pitted

¾ cup plant-based or dairy milk

2 tablespoons lemon juice

2 teaspoons vanilla extract

1¾ cups spelt flour or flour of choice

7 tablespoons raw cacao powder or cocoa powder

1 teaspoon baking soda

1 teaspoon baking powder

¾ teaspoon salt, or more to taste

⅓ cup coconut oil or butter, melted, plus extra for greasing

¾ cup coconut sugar

3 medium organic eggs, or 3 bananas, mashed

CHOCOLATE CASHEW BUTTER CREAM:

1⅔ cups raw cashew nuts, presoaked in warm water for an hour, then drained

6 tablespoons cashew or other plant-based milk

3 tablespoons agave syrup

2 tablespoons raw cacao or cocoa powder

1 teaspoon vanilla extract

pinch of salt

LINGONBERRY GLAZE

6 tablespoons coconut milk

2 tablespoons lingonberry powder (can be substituted with other flavoring powder or smooth berry puree)

5 tablespoons agave syrup

2 teaspoons vanilla extract

6 tablespoons coconut oil

**I prefer moderately sweetened desserts to sugar bombs. I like to "cut" the sweetness with grown-up flavors such as nuts, coffee, and, as in this recipe, earthy beet, which gives a deep, juicy tone to this take on a red velvet cake. The cacao or cocoa and beet are balanced by the modest sweetness of the dates and coconut sugar, and a luscious lingonberry glaze to continue the velvet theme. This is a beautiful cake to serve at any time of year.**

Preheat the oven to 350°F. Grease an 8-inch round cake pan with coconut oil or butter and line the bottom with parchment paper.

Put the beets, dates, milk, lemon juice, and vanilla in a food processor and process until smooth. Sift together the flour, cacao or cocoa powder, baking soda, baking powder, and salt into a bowl and set aside.

Using a handheld mixer or a balloon whisk, beat together the coconut oil or butter and coconut sugar in a large bowl until smooth. Add the eggs one by one, or add the bananas (or other egg replacer) a third at a time, beating well after each addition. Combine the beet mixture, flour mixture, and coconut oil or butter mixture, adding a small quantity of each mixture at a time to a separate large bowl while beating constantly. Pour the batter into the prepared pan and bake for 60 minutes or until a skewer inserted into the center of the cake comes out clean. Remove from the oven and allow to cool in the pan. To make the chocolate cashew butter cream, combine all the ingredients in a food processor and process until smooth. Cover and refrigerate until ready to use. It will keep in the fridge for 2 days.

Meanwhile, prepare the lingonberry glaze. Mix the glaze ingredients, except the coconut oil, in a blender until smooth. Add the coconut oil, a tablespoon at a time, and blend until smooth.

To assemble, remove the cake from its pan and peel away the parchment paper, then place on a serving platter. Carefully halve the cake horizontally and set the top aside. Using a flat spatula, spread the cashew butter cream evenly over the bottom cake layer. Place the top half over the cashew butter cream and drizzle with the lingonberry glaze.

**VE** Opt for plant-based milk, coconut oil, and vegan egg replacer.

**GF** The cake is not gluten-free.

### Lingonberry powder

*Lingonberry powder is made with lingonberries and has emerged recently as an exciting powder to use in desserts and other dishes where sour, tangy flavor is needed. Lingonberries are a popular ingredient in Scandinavian cooking and the dried powder is a popular choice in place of Brazilian açaí powder when making smoothies.*

# 4. CELEBRATION SALADS

Salads were once the mere sideshow of the dining experience, but not anymore. As these recipes demonstrate, salads have now moved center stage to become star dishes in their own right, exploding with flavor, color, and texture. Dressings are key to creating a great salad, with their ability to bring out the full flavor of ingredients and also to bring them together. But they perform a fine balancing act between mellow and tangy, salty and sweet, so always adjust the components to your taste before serving.
Salads invite you to be flexible, so adopt the traditional Japanese wabi-sabi approach of going with the natural flow and making the best of what you've got. So if you're missing an ingredient or two, simply substitute ones that have similar qualities, for example sweetness, crispiness, or fresh fragrance.

# Sweet Potatoes, Kale, and Spicy Chickpeas with Lemon Almond Dressing

SERVES 4

**SWEET POTATOES AND SPICY CHICKPEAS:**

1 medium sweet potato, peeled and cut into small wedges

2 tablespoons olive oil

salt, to taste

½ teaspoon ground cumin

1 (14-ounce) can chickpeas, drained and patted dry with paper towels

½ teaspoon sweet paprika

¼ teaspoon red pepper flakes

**KALE:**

olive oil, for frying

2½ ounces kale or cavolo nero (black kale), stalks removed and chopped

salt and freshly ground black pepper, to taste

**LEMON ALMOND DRESSING:**

½ cup plus 2 tablespoons nut or seed milk

3 tablespoons almond butter

2 tablespoons shoyu soy sauce or tamari

1 teaspoon lemon juice

2 garlic cloves

1 teaspoon honey or agave syrup

½ teaspoon crushed garlic (or grated fresh ginger for a variation)

**TO SERVE:**

3 tablespoons pomegranate seeds

2½ ounces baby spinach leaves

2 carrots, julienned

½ red onion, sliced

2 slices of radish, to garnish (optional)

**This filling salad offers a variety of flavors and textures. Wilted kale and meltingly soft sweet potato make a great combination, with spicy roasted chickpeas. Finished with pomegranate seeds, avocado, and red onion, this sumptuous salad covers all the bases.**

Preheat the oven to 450°F and line one or two baking sheets with parchment paper. Toss the sweet potato wedges with 1 tablespoon of the olive oil, a sprinkle of salt, and the cumin in a bowl until well mixed. In a separate bowl, toss the chickpeas with the remaining 1 tablespoon olive oil, the paprika, and the red pepper flakes. Arrange the sweet potato wedges and chickpeas separately in a single layer on the lined baking sheet (use two sheets if necessary) and roast for 30 minutes.

Heat a skillet over medium-high heat. Add a drizzle of olive oil and fry the kale or cavolo nero until wilted. Sprinkle with a little salt and pepper.

Combine all the ingredients for the lemon almond dressing in a pitcher and blend with an immersion blender until well combined.

In a large serving bowl, combine everything and serve with the lemon almond dressing.

**VE** Opt for agave syrup.
**GF** Opt for gluten-free tamari.

# Mint Avocado Smoothie

**Give green smoothies a mint edge!**

SERVES 1
1 avocado, chopped
2 tablespoons almond butter
2 Medjool dates, pitted
2 teaspoons chlorella or wheatgrass
3 tablespoons chopped fresh mint
1 cup fresh spinach
¾ cup plant-based milk
pinch of salt

Blend all the ingredients in a food processor until smooth, adding a little more plant-based milk if you want a thinner consistency.

VE ✓ GF ✓

# Beet Carrot Smoothie

**Beet blends deliciously with raspberries and carrot. I use raspberries to freshen up the flavor of the beet, but you can use other berries.**

SERVES 1
½ medium carrot
1 small red beet, peeled and
   finely grated
150ml plant-based milk
50g raspberries
50g presoaked cashew nuts
1 Medjool date, pitted
pinch of salt

Blend all the ingredients in a food processor until smooth, adding a little more plant-based milk if you want a thinner consistency.

VE ✓ GF ✓

# Cauliflower Smoothie

**Cauli and turmeric, dates and ginger make this golden smoothie stand out.**

SERVES 1
1¾ ounces cauliflower florets
1 ripe small banana
2 Medjool dates, pitted
1 teaspoon ground or fresh turmeric
pinch of freshly ground black pepper
¼ teaspoon ground cinnamon
½ teaspoon ground or fresh ginger
¾ cup coconut or other plant-based milk

Blend all the ingredients in a food processor until smooth, adding a little more plant-based milk if you want a thinner consistency.

VE ✓ GF ✓

# New Moon Salad

In mindfulness and yoga, the new moon represents a time to start anew and many people eat nourishing and cleansing foods during this time. This salad is filled with protein-rich quinoa and healthy fats from walnuts and avocado. If you want the full health bar experience, serve with nourishing smoothies or fresh juices.

SERVES 4
1¼ cups quinoa, rinsed
7 ounces your favorite beans (I used
   cooked edamame and black beans)
2 avocados, sliced
1¾ ounces radishes, any variety, thinly
   sliced
2 handfuls of mixed sprouts and
   microgreens (I use bean sprouts,
   beet and radish sprouts, and green
   microgreens)
1 cup baby spinach leaves
2 medium carrots, julienned
2 handfuls of walnuts

NEW MOON DRESSING:
1 teaspoon chlorella or wheatgrass
3 tablespoons chopped fresh cilantro
1 garlic clove, crushed
½ teaspoon salt
1 tablespoon nutritional yeast
1 teaspoon lemon or lime juice
1 tablespoon olive oil or other cold-
   pressed oil
1 teaspoon honey or agave syrup
3½ ounces crème fraîche or vegan crème
   fraîche or Greek yogurt

Put the quinoa in a saucepan and add double the amount of water to the quinoa. Cook for 15 minutes, drain, and cool. Mix the ingredients for the dressing together. Divide the quinoa and the rest of the salad ingredients between bowls or arrange in one large serving bowl. Serve with a drizzle of the dressing.

VE Use vegan crème fraîche. GF ✓

# Farmer's Market and Noodle Salad

SERVES 4

vegetable oil, for frying

10½ ounces firm organic tofu, drained and pressed, cut into bite-size pieces

2 tablespoons shoyu soy sauce or tamari

2 tablespoons agave syrup

¼ teaspoon ground chile powder

14 ounces mixed vegetables, such as carrots, cabbage (I use bok choy), kale or cavolo nero (black kale), broccoli, cauliflower, or green beans, peeled and stalks removed where necessary and separated into florets or cut into bite-size pieces

9 ounces dried noodles of your choice

2 handfuls of fresh bean sprouts or other sprouts

a handful of fresh cilantro, chopped

2 tablespoons sesame seeds

salt and freshly ground black pepper, to taste

SOY AND CHILE DRESSING:

6 tablespoons shoyu soy sauce or tamari

2 tablespoons toasted sesame oil

1 garlic clove, crushed

2 tablespoons almond or cashew butter

2 tablespoons gochujang, chile paste, sriracha, or other hot sauce

juice of 1 lime

2 teaspoons coconut sugar

**When you're planning to cook for a gathering, it can be tricky if you have a strict ingredient list to shop for because if you can't get a hold of key ingredients, despite their being in season, you're faced with replanning a whole meal at the last minute. The solution is to rely on pantry staples such as noodles as a base, and reliable flavorings for making sauces that you can easily customize to work with whatever fresh vegetables are available on the day. I love farmer's markets where I can source both exceptional fresh organic ingredients, such as beautiful broccoli, cabbage, and carrots, along with other top-quality ingredients to keep in store. This Asian-inspired market salad, a sprouted version of Pad Thai, uses a feisty soy sauce dressing to bring added flavor to mixed fresh vegetables of your choice. Top with crunchy bean sprouts for extra textural interest.**

Heat a skillet over medium-high heat. Add a drizzle of vegetable oil and fry the tofu until golden brown on all sides, 2 to 3 minutes. Mix the soy sauce, agave, and chile powder and splash the mixture on the tofu. Fry for a minute and remove from the heat. Season to taste with salt and pepper and let cool.

Prepare the vegetables that need to be cooked. If using broccoli or cauliflower florets, steam them for 4 minutes. If using sturdy greens, such as kale or cavolo nero, fry in a little drizzle of oil over medium-high heat for 1 to 2 minutes until wilted. Green beans can be steamed as for the broccoli or cauliflower or blanched in boiling water for 1 minute. Allow to cool.

Cook the noodles according to the package instructions, then drain and rinse in cold water. Meanwhile, combine all the ingredients for the soy and chile dressing in a pitcher and blend with an immersion blender until well combined. Divide the noodles among serving plates or bowls with the prepared veggies and tofu. Add the sprouts and cilantro, and drizzle with the soy and chile dressing. Sprinkle with sesame seeds and serve.

VE Use egg-free noodles.

GF Opt for gluten-free tamari and sriracha or another gluten-free hot sauce; use gluten-free noodles such as buckwheat soba noodles.

# Wabi-Sabi Salad

SERVES 4

1 cup brown rice or Japanese or sushi rice

vegetable oil or ghee, for frying

7 ounces oyster or shiitake mushrooms, sliced

½ teaspoon shichimi togarashi or red pepper flakes

9 ounces freshly shelled edamame beans

2 tablespoons furikake (see page 166 for homemade)

7 ounces firm smoked tofu, cut into matchsticks

1 to 2 watermelon radishes or Chioggia beets, trimmed, peeled, and cut into thin sticks

2 carrots, cut into matchsticks

½ dragon fruit, flesh scooped out and diced

1 avocado, diced

WABI-SABI SAUCE:

3 tablespoons shoyu soy sauce or tamari

3 tablespoons rice vinegar

1 teaspoon honey or agave syrup

1 teaspoon grated fresh ginger

1 tablespoon almond or cashew butter

1 tablespoon sesame oil

1 teaspoon nutritional yeast, or 1 garlic clove, crushed (optional)

TO GARNISH:

black sesame seeds

ready-toasted nori, cut into thin strips

This salad is a fun and delicious way to enjoy the essence of sushi for those who love it but don't love the bother of rolling nori sheets. Wabi-sabi is a traditional Japanese philosophy that celebrates the beauty of imperfection, so in that spirit, feel free to change and customize your salad using different vegetables and grains. I've added mushrooms, which fall outside of the usual sushi flavor palette but deliver a umami boost to the dish.

The sauce and furikake (if you make your own) can be prepared a day or a few hours ahead of serving. The rice can be cooked, cooled, and stored in a sealed container in the fridge up to a day ahead. Cut the vegetables just before assembly.

———

Prepare and cook the rice according to the package instructions (or according to the instructions on page 16, if using Japanese or sushi rice), then drain if necessary and let cool.

Meanwhile, heat a skillet over medium-high heat. Add a drizzle of vegetable oil and fry the oyster mushrooms, leaving them undisturbed, for 2 minutes, then fry, stirring, for 5 minutes or until they have shrunk in size and the excess moisture has evaporated. Sprinkle with the shichimi togarashi or red pepper flakes. Cook the edamame beans in a saucepan of boiling water for 3 to 5 minutes until tender. Drain and fresh under cold running water.

Combine all the ingredients for the wabi-sabi sauce in a pitcher and blend with an immersion blender until well combined.

Transfer the cooled cooked rice to a large serving bowl, then mix the furikake into the rice. Arrange all the prepared ingredients in a bowl and garnish with black sesame seeds and nori strips before serving with the wabi-sabi sauce.

### Tip

*Add ¼ teaspoon wasabi paste to the sauce for a hot variation.*

VE Make your own furikake (see page 166) or look for fish-free furikake if buying ready-made; opt for agave syrup.

GF Opt for gluten-free tamari.

# Watermelon and Chioggia Beets with Miso Wow Sauce

SERVES 4

1 to 2 Chioggia beets, peeled, thinly
    sliced, and cut to bite-size triangles
7 ounces watermelon flesh, cut into
    bite-size triangles

MISO WOW SAUCE

1½ tablespoons red miso paste or brown
    rice miso paste (genmai)
1½ teaspoons drained capers
1 tablespoon shoyu soy sauce or tamari
1 teaspoon lemon juice
⅓ teaspoon honey or agave syrup
2 tablespoons nutritional yeast or
    grated Parmesan
6 tablespoons water
1 teaspoon kuzu (optional)
¼ teaspoon freshly ground black pepper
3½ ounces mayonnaise or crème fraîche
1 tablespoon microgreens, such as red
    vein sorrel leaves and shiso leaves,
    or delicate herbs, such as baby basil
    leaves, to garnish
1 teaspoon black sesame seeds, to
    garnish

**This vibrant sharing salad combines sweet watermelon with earthy Chioggia beets and offers fresh sweet and savory flavors to tease the appetite. But it's actually the sauce that's the real star in this ensemble. You can use this creamy miso sauce warm or cold with any variety of cooked or raw vegetables. I call it Miso Wow Sauce!**

To make the sauce, put all the sauce ingredients, except the mayonnaise or crème fraîche, in a food processor and process until smooth. Transfer to a small saucepan and bring to a boil, stirring, then turn off the heat. Let cool slightly, then whisk in the mayonnaise or crème fraîche. The sauce can be made a day in advance and kept, tightly covered or in an airtight container, in the fridge. Before serving, heat up the sauce, whisking it until smooth and adding a little water to loosen the consistency if necessary. Let cool slightly before serving.

Arrange the Chioggia beet and watermelon slices on a serving dish, drizzle with the sauce, and top with microgreens and black sesame seeds.

**VE** Opt for vegan mayonnaise or vegan
crème fraîche; use agave syrup and
nutritional yeast.
**GF** Opt for gluten-free tamari.

Tip
*I've used kuzu here as a thickener, which gives a lovely smoothness and shine to sauces and gels without any weird aftertaste, but you can use arrowroot starch or another thickener if you prefer. Alternatively, add vegan or dairy crème fraîche to the sauce instead.*

# Pea Shoots and Zucchini Salad with Hot Tamari Tempeh

SERVES 4

9 ounces best-quality tempeh, cut into
    bite-size pieces
vegetable oil, for frying

DRESSING:

5 tablespoons shoyu soy sauce or tamari
2 tablespoons mirin
2 tablespoons rice vinegar
1½ teaspoons grated fresh ginger
1 tablespoon coconut sugar or agave syrup
¼ teaspoon salt

TEMPEH SEASONING:

2 tablespoons shoyu soy sauce or tamari
1 tablespoon coconut sugar or agave syrup
1 teaspoon sriracha or other hot sauce

4 scallions, chopped
½ cucumber, chopped
1 large avocado, sliced
2 medium zucchini, spiralized
a handful of pea shoots

This very fresh and cool salad combines spiralized zucchini with cucumber, avocado, scallions, and tender raw pea shoots. It's a perfect spring and summer salad, but also an option to complement heartier dishes when you need to balance them with something less heavy. The tempeh adds a spicy flavor and extra interest to the salad. A light and sweetened tamari and ginger dressing gives an extra edge to the taste. You can use other delicate shoots or sprouts instead of pea shoots and use tofu or chickpeas instead of tempeh.

Mix the ingredients for the dressing together and set aside. Mix the ingredients for the tempeh seasoning together and set aside.

Heat a skillet over medium-high heat. Add a drizzle of vegetable oil and fry the tempeh, letting the pieces fry until the surface is seared and golden before stirring and turning the pieces around, 4 to 5 minutes. When the tempeh is nicely golden on all sides, splash the seasoning mixture over the pieces and allow the liquid to be absorbed before removing the tempeh from the heat.

Divide the salad among individual serving bowls or mix the ingredients in one large bowl. Serve with the tempeh and dressing.

VE ✓
GF Opt for gluten-free tamari.

# Nordic
# Nacho Salad

SERVES 4

COTTAGE CHEESE AND
   HORSERADISH DIP:

1 tablespoon horseradish sauce, plus
   more to taste (or use 1 teaspoon chile
   paste or wasabi paste)

¼ teaspoon salt, plus more to taste

1 tablespoon olive oil

100g cottage cheese

1 tablespoon lemon juice

4 tortillas or flatbreads of choice (you can
   also use thin Swedish crispbreads—
   they don't need toasting)

75g baby spinach or other greens

9 ounces chanterelles or other
   mushrooms

olive oil or butter, for frying

3 tablespoons minced chives

salt and freshly ground black pepper

**VE** Use vegan soft cheese or vegan crème fraîche
instead of cottage cheese.
**GF** Opt for corn, not wheat, tortillas or use
gluten-free flatbreads or crackers.

**Chanterelles are highly rated in Scandinavia and mostly prepared in a simple manner to let the pure flavor sing. In this salad, fried chanterelles are layered with spinach, chives, and a zesty horseradish cream. For a crispy contrast, toasted tortillas or flatbread adds a crunch to the dish; if you want to go the whole way with the Scandinavian theme, you can use thin knäckebröd (Swedish crispbread), like the sesame and sea salt cracker from the brand Wasa.**

Mix the ingredients for the dip until smooth. Cut the tortilla into smaller pieces. Heat a skillet and toast the tortilla pieces until crispy on both sides, 20 to 30 seconds on each side. Remove and place on a serving plate with the spinach.

Heat the skillet over medium-high heat and add the chanterelles without any fat. Fry the chanterelles, stirring every few seconds, until they release their liquid. When the liquids have reduced in the pan, add a drizzle of olive oil or a tablespoon of butter and fry quickly to coat, sprinkle with salt and pepper, and transfer to the serving plate. Dot with the cottage cheese and horseradish dip so that it is evenly distributed. Sprinkle with chives, season with and pepper to taste, and serve.

# Pumpkin, Wild Rice, and Lemongrass Salad

SERVES 4

1¼ cups wild rice

1 medium pumpkin or Delicata squash, halved, seeds and membrane removed, peeled, and cut into wedges

peanut or vegetable oil, for drizzling

⅓ cup toasted hazelnuts

2 avocados, sliced

a handful of mixed cilantro and flat-leaf parsley leaves

salt and freshly ground black pepper, to taste

LEMONGRASS DRESSING:

6 tablespoons rice vinegar

2 tablespoons shoyu soy sauce or tamari

1 tablespoon toasted sesame oil

1 teaspoon fresh lime juice

2 tablespoons coconut sugar

1 lemongrass stalk, white part only, tough outer layers removed, finely chopped

1 garlic clove, crushed

1 teaspoon grated fresh ginger

1 teaspoon minced red chile

salt, to taste

TO SERVE

lime wedges

shiso leaves or other microgreens (optional)

VE ✓

GF Opt for gluten-free tamari.

**Here is a salad full of dramatic contrasts. Sweet roasted pumpkin or squash wedges are enhanced by a tangy Asian-style lemongrass dressing, with wild rice providing a striking black color and chewy texture. Wild rice has to be dried and roasted before it's edible and this process gives the grains their extra-deep nutty flavor and hue. It's often sold mixed with regular long-grain rice, sometimes with the addition of gluten-containing flavorings, so check the details on the package for gluten content and cooking time. Toasted hazelnuts add a harmonizing element to finish.**

Cook the wild rice according to the package instructions (usually simmered for about 45 minutes), then drain.

Preheat the oven to 400°F. Line a baking sheet with parchment paper. Put the pumpkin or squash wedges in a bowl, drizzle with oil, and sprinkle with salt and pepper, then toss to coat. Arrange in a single layer on the lined baking sheet and roast for 25 minutes. Flip the wedges over and roast on the other side for 10 minutes or until golden and tender.

Meanwhile, whisk together all the ingredients for the lemongrass dressing in a bowl until well combined.

To serve, toss the roasted pumpkin or squash with the cooked wild rice, top with the toasted hazelnuts, avocado, and herbs, and drizzle with the lemongrass dressing. Serve warm with lime wedges for squeezing and shiso leaves, if you wish.

# Jackfruit Bulgogi Salad

SERVES 4

2 tablespoons toasted sesame oil

2 tablespoons rice vinegar or citrus juice

salt and freshly ground black pepper,
    to taste

14 ounces Jackfruit Bulgogi (see page
    125)

2 avocados, diced

1 Asian pear or regular firm pear, cored
    and cut into strips

4 scallions, sliced

3 cups baby spinach or other tender
    greens

6 tablespoons toasted cashews

1 tablespoon sesame seeds

**This salad is packed with flavor! Using fried jackfruit, marinated with shoyu and chile, as a delicious savory element in a fresh green salad. Pear, avocado, and spinach add a cool contrast and cashews lend the extra crunch. The bulgogi is best served warm, but you can eat this salad warm or cold. It's an excellent dish to take to a barbecue or potluck supper.**

Mix the toasted sesame oil and rice vinegar together and set aside. Arrange the rest of the ingredients in a bowl and serve with the dressing.

**VE** ✓

**GF** Opt for tamari when preparing the Jackfruit Bulgogi.

# Herbed Beet, Lentil, and Feta Salad

SERVES 4

4 medium beets, washed
8 small carrots, scrubbed and sliced
    lengthwise
olive oil, for roasting
1 tablespoon fresh thyme leaves
4 cups vegetable stock or water
2 handfuls of baby spinach leaves
7 ounces feta or soft fresh goat's cheese
a handful of tarragon leaves,
    minced
extra-virgin olive oil, for drizzling
7 ounces Puy lentils, rinsed and drained
salt and freshly ground black pepper,
    to taste

DIJON DRESSING:

3 tablespoons olive oil
2 tablespoons red vine vinegar
1 tablespoon mayonnaise
1 teaspoon Dijon mustard
1 teaspoon honey or agave syrup
2 garlic cloves, crushed
1 teaspoon fresh thyme leaves
½ teaspoon salt
freshly ground black pepper, to taste

**I like to combine earthy-tasting lentils and beet with bold flavors, here with a mustard-spiked dressing and tangy cheese. There's a French thread running through the ingredients in this salad, from the Dijon mustard to the Puy lentils and the tarragon and aromatic fresh thyme, but it's a dish that blends easily with other dishes for sharing or as a side dish, as well as being sufficiently substantial to be served as a main.**

Preheat the oven to 400°F. Wrap the beets individually in foil and set them on a baking sheet. Put the carrots in a bowl, drizzle with olive oil and sprinkle with salt, then toss to coat. Transfer to the baking sheet and sprinkle with the thyme. Roast for about 45 minutes or until the beets are tender, but keep an eye on the carrots and remove them from the oven earlier if they look done. Let the beets and carrots cool, then peel the beets and cut them into small wedges.

Meanwhile, bring the stock or water to a boil in a saucepan. Add the lentils, reduce the heat, and simmer gently for 20 to 25 minutes until tender. Drain and rinse in cold water. Shake off the excess moisture and let air-dry for a few minutes.

Whisk together all the ingredients for the Dijon dressing in a bowl until well combined.

Tip the lentils into a large serving bowl, drizzle with the dressing, and season to taste with salt and pepper. Add the baby spinach and the roasted beets and carrots, then crumble the cheese over the top. Sprinkle with the tarragon and add a drizzle of extra-virgin olive oil.

**VE** Opt for vegan feta-style or soft cheese,
vegan mayonnaise, and agave syrup.
**GF** Opt for gluten-free mayonnaise.

# Strawberry Summer Salad

SERVES 4

9 ounces cherry tomatoes, chopped

1 small red onion, diced small

3 cups salad greens

3½ ounces strawberries, halved

½ cup toasted nuts, such as walnuts, pecans, or almonds

1 avocado, cut into small pieces

1½ cups croutons

DRESSING:

3 tablespoons balsamic vinegar

2 garlic cloves, crushed and mashed into a paste with ¾ teaspoon salt

1½ teaspoons honey or agave syrup or other sweetener

3 tablespoons extra-virgin olive oil

1 teaspoon Dijon mustard

**I make this salad as soon as there are fresh strawberries in season. It's the perfect side dish that goes well with literally anything savory. Adding strawberries to a regular green salad with tomatoes makes it instantly festive. The sweet berries add a lovely contrast to garlic and onions, while croutons and nuts give a pleasing crunch. In the winter, swap the strawberries for dried fruit, such as apricots, figs, or raisins.**

———

Mix the dressing ingredients together in a large bowl. Add the tomatoes and red onion and toss to coat. Let sit for 20 minutes or longer. Toss with the rest of the ingredients and serve.

**VE** Opt for agave syrup.

**GF** Opt for gluten-free croutons, or omit them.

# 5. HEARTY MEALS

Stews, curries, and bakes are perfect choices for gatherings—fuss-free and brimming
with melding flavors as a result of all the ingredients being cooked together
in the pot or dish. The cooking methods involved also contribute to a satisfying taste
experience, with vegetables releasing an abundance of flavor when roasted in
the oven or slow-cooked on the stovetop.

With these recipes, you can treat your guests to vegetable-enriched takes on
hearty classics from around the globe, including a sweet and fragrant
Tunisian stew of eggplants and tomatoes, and a rainbow-colored
feast of curry dishes. This is comfort food at its best!

# Golden Kerala Curry

SERVES 4 TO 6

2¼ pounds mixed vegetables, such as
    peppers, baby eggplant, green beans,
    and zucchini, chopped or sliced
ghee or vegetable oil, for frying
4 shallots, minced
2 cups vegetable stock
3¼ cups coconut milk
3 tablespoons light soy sauce or tamari
1½ tablespoons coconut or brown sugar
a handful of cilantro, chopped

SPICE PASTE:
1 tablespoon ghee or coconut oil
5 garlic cloves, crushed
2 teaspoons fresh lemongrass or
    lemongrass paste
½ red chile, seeded, or more to taste
1 tablespoon grated fresh ginger
¾ tablespoon ground turmeric
2 teaspoons garam masala
1 teaspoon ground coriander
¼ teaspoon freshly ground black pepper
¾ tablespoon salt, plus more to taste

TO SERVE:
fresh cilantro
2 cups cooked rice or other grain
1 to 2 limes, cut into wedges
yogurt or raita
naan

**Inspired by the flavors of Kerala, the region of South India known for its many Ayurvedic and yoga schools and for being one of the happiest places on earth, according to some studies, this is a stew for nourishing mind, body, and spirit! Light and satisfying at the same time, it is flavored with coconut, turmeric, and lemongrass. Don't be deterred by the long list of ingredients, as most are spices or pantry staples you probably already have at home. You can choose to make the curry less or more spicy. Add ½ red chile to start, then add more as you like for extra heat.**

**The Indian Carrot Salad (see page 101) makes a perfect side dish for this stew, but raita and naan bread work well, too.**

Put all the ingredients for the spice paste in a food processor and process to a coarse paste. Rub the paste all over the prepared mixed vegetables.

Heat a large heavy-bottomed saucepan or casserole over medium heat. Add a little ghee or a drizzle of vegetable oil and fry the shallots, stirring, for 4 to 5 minutes until translucent. Add the vegetables with all the spice paste and a little more ghee or oil, then fry, stirring, for 2 to 3 minutes. Stir in the stock, coconut milk, soy sauce, and sugar and bring to a boil, then reduce the heat and simmer for 15 minutes. Taste and adjust the seasoning with salt, if needed.

Sprinkle cilantro over the curry and serve with cooked rice or other grain, along with lime wedges, either yogurt or raita, and naan.

**VE** Opt for coconut oil for the spice paste and
vegetable oil for frying; use vegan yogurt.
**GF** Opt for gluten-free tamari. Serve with
gluten-free flatbread instead of naan.

# Rainbow Curry Table

**PILAF:**

1¼ cups basmati rice, rinsed in several changes of cold water until the water is clear, then soaked in fresh cold water for 30 minutes

2 cups water

1 chai tea bag

ghee or vegetable oil, for frying

2 shallots, finely sliced

1 teaspoon ground turmeric

½ teaspoon ground cinnamon

¼ teaspoon freshly ground black pepper

6 tablespoons toasted almonds, coarsely ground

2 garlic cloves, crushed

a handful of raisins

**CHICKPEA AND SPINACH CURRY:**

ghee or vegetable oil, for frying

2 shallots, finely diced

2 teapoons black mustard seeds, toasted and ground

1 tablespoon ground coriander

¾ tablespoon garam masala

¾ teaspoon salt, plus extra to taste

10½ ounces spinach, coarsely chopped

2 (14-ounce) cans chickpeas, rinsed and drained

2½ cups vegetable stock

¼ cup fresh cilantro, minced

1 tablespoon lemon juice

1 teaspoon honey or agave syrup

**SIMPLE RAITA:**

7 ounces yogurt

pinch of salt

pinch of cumin

2 tablespoons grated cucumber (optional)

**TO SERVE:**

Tandoori Cauliflower (see page 101)

Cherry Chutney (see page 131)

pickles

naan bread

Comforting and full of vibrant flavor, curries win my heart and my stomach every time! The concept of this meal is to serve a table of curries, where the flavors of the different dishes fold into one another beautifully when combined in each guest's bowl. Alternatively, you can cherry pick any one of the components to make and enjoy on its own.

The bold smoky quality of the tandoori cauliflower harmonizes well with the fragrant lemony edge of the fresh cilantro in the chickpea and spinach curry, while the pilaf is made warmly aromatic and earthy with the spicing of chai tea and therapeutic turmeric.

Take your guests further on the spice trail by adding cherry chutney (see page 131), a fantastic sweet contrast to the savory curry, and cooling elements to complete the taste experience, such as a tangy yogurt raita, pickles, and naan bread.

To make the pilaf, drain the rice and put it in a saucepan that has a tight-fitting lid, cover with the 2 cups water, and add the tea bag. Bring to a boil, then reduce the heat, cover the pan with the lid, and simmer for 10 to 12 minutes. Turn off the heat, remove the tea bag, and leave the rice to stand, uncovered, while you fry the shallots.

Heat a large, wide skillet over medium heat. Add a little ghee or vegetable oil and fry the shallots, stirring frequently, for 5 to 7 minutes until transparent. Add the remaining pilaf ingredients including the cooked rice and fry, stirring, for 3 to 4 minutes.

To make the chickpea and spinach curry, heat a saucepan that has a lid over medium-high heat. Add a little ghee or vegetable oil and fry the shallots with the spices and salt, stirring, for 4 to 5 minutes. Add the spinach and cook, stirring it with the shallot and spices, until wilted. Stir in the remaining curry ingredients, cover the pan with the lid, and simmer for 10 minutes. Taste and adjust the seasoning with salt.

To make the raita, simply mix the raita ingredients together in a small bowl.

To assemble the curry table, put the warm pilaf and chickpea and spinach curry in separate serving dishes, along with accompanying dishes of the Tandoori Cauliflower and Cherry Chutney, plus raita, pickles, and naan bread.

**VE** Opt for vegetable oil for frying and agave syrup for the curry; opt for vegan yogurt for making the Tandoori Cauliflower and raita.

**GF** Serve with gluten-free flatbread instead of naan.

# Tandoori Cauliflower

This dish of mouth-watering cauliflower is coated with a tandoori yogurt marinade spiked with sweet and smoked paprika before baking for an extra depth of flavor. Serve as a side with other curries. Alternatively, turn it into a main meal for four by serving with rice or pilaf (see page 99) and other Indian side dishes such as pickles, raita, and naan bread.

SERVES 8

1 cauliflower, divided into florets

TANDOORI YOGURT MARINADE:

1¼ cups Greek yogurt
6 tablespoons olive oil
2 tablespoons sweet paprika
1 teaspoon smoked paprika
1 tablespoon plus 1 teaspoon garam masala
2 teaspoons ground turmeric
1 teaspoon salt, plus extra to taste
2 teaspoons agave syrup
¼ teaspoon cayenne pepper, or more to taste

Preheat the oven to 400°F. Whisk together all the ingredients for the tandoori yogurt marinade in a bowl until smooth. Rub the cauliflower florets with half the marinade and arrange them in a single layer in a large ovenproof dish. Bake for 45 to 50 minutes.

Toward the end of the baking time, gently heat the remainder of the marinade in a saucepan. When the cauliflower is done, pour the warmed-up marinade over the florets and season to taste with salt and cayenne pepper. The tandoori marinade can be prepared a day ahead and kept, tightly covered, in the fridge.

**VE** Opt for vegan yogurt.
**GF** ✓

# Indian Carrot Salad

This dish always attracts praise around the table. It's delicious with curries, but will bring a cooling, sweet contrast to many other types of savory dish. I use baby orange carrots, or rainbow carrots if I can find them.

SERVES 4 TO 6

1 pound good-quality carrots, peeled
1 to 2 avocados, cut into wedges
1 small red onion, thinly sliced
a handful of fresh cilantro
a handful of mint
a handful of sesame seeds
salt and freshly ground black pepper, to taste

DRESSING:

2½ tablespoons rice vinegar or white wine vinegar
1 tablespoon extra-virgin olive oil
1 tablespoon toasted sesame oil
1 garlic clove, crushed
1 teaspoon grated fresh ginger
1 teaspoon ground cumin
½ teaspoon ground coriander

Slice the carrots lengthwise into thin ribbons. Arrange the ribbons in a serving dish with the avocado, onion, and herbs, then sprinkle with salt and pepper to taste.

Whisk together all the dressing ingredients in a small bowl until smooth, then pour over the salad. Sprinkle with the sesame seeds.

**VE** ✓ **GF** ✓

# Ribollita

SERVES 4

olive oil, for frying

5 shallots, minced

3 garlic cloves, minced

2 carrots, finely diced

1 celery stick, finely chopped

pinch of ground fennel seeds

1 tablespoon dried rosemary or thyme,
    or a pinch of red pepper flakes

¾ teaspoon salt

7 ounces cavolo nero (black
    kale), stems removed and leaves
    finely chopped

¼ cup flat-leaf parsley, minced

1 quart good-quality vegetable stock

3 tablespoons red wine

1 teaspoon honey or agave syrup

2 tablespoons grated Parmesan or
    rawmesan (see page 28)

1 (14-ounce) can good-quality plum
    tomatoes

1 (14-ounce) can cannellini beans, rinsed
    and drained

extra-virgin olive oil, for drizzling

salt and freshly ground black pepper,
    to taste

TO SERVE

7 ounces dry bread, torn into chunks
    (optional)

**Ribollita is a well-rounded flavor affair, and one of my all-time favorite dishes. The star ingredient here is cavolo nero, a black kale with a deep baritone taste that makes a perfect contrast to tomatoes, bread and beans in this rustic Tuscan farmers' soup. Though filling, it's guaranteed to make your friends and family ask for a second serving. Scoop up!**

Heat a large saucepan over medium-high heat. Add a drizzle of olive oil and fry the onions, garlic, carrots, and celery with the spices and salt for 3 to 4 minutes, stirring. Add the cavolo nero and fry, stirring, until wilted. Add all the remaining ingredients except the beans and the extra-virgin olive oil, stir well, and simmer for 15 minutes.

Add the beans and a drizzle of extra-virgin olive oil, then taste and adjust the seasoning with salt and pepper. Serve hot.

## Tip

*Serve the ribollita with some good rustic bread, gluten-free if required.*

**VE** Opt for agave syrup and rawmesan (see page 28).

**GF** Omit the bread or opt for gluten-free bread.

*Facing page: Roasted
Baby Pumpkin (page 115).*

# Garlic Mushrooms and Cavolo Nero with Red Rice and Fried Eggs

SERVES 4

1 cup red rice, or other whole grain rice

olive oil, for frying

10½ ounces chestnut mushrooms, sliced

4 garlic cloves, minced

5¼ ounces cavolo nero (black kale), stalks removed and leaves finely chopped

a handful of flat-leaf parsley, coarsely chopped, plus extra to serve

2 tablespoons nutritional yeast or grated Parmesan (optional)

salt and freshly ground black pepper, to taste

TO SERVE:

4 fried medium organic eggs

lemon wedges

2 small avocados, sliced

**Rice dishes like risottos and paellas are perfect for big gatherings and small budgets, where you can combine a variety of ingredients with rice to cook conveniently together in one pan. For this dish, you only have to cook the rice ahead in a separate pan, which requires less attention and stirring from you than a risotto or paella. I'm using red rice, which gives a nutty flavor, but you can use other varieties, such as brown, black, or basmati. This dish is filling and quick and you can cook the recipe a day ahead.**

Cook the rice according to the instructions on the package (for red rice, around 45 minutes). Set aside.

Add a drizzle of oil to a pan over high heat and fry the mushrooms, stirring gently, for 2 minutes. Reduce the heat to medium and fry for an additional 2 to 3 minutes or until the excess moisture has reduced. Reserve a few of the prettiest mushrooms for garnish.

Add another drizzle of oil, the garlic, and the cavolo nero, increase the heat to medium-high again, and fry, stirring, for 1 to 2 minutes until the cavolo nero is wilted. Return all the remaining main ingredients and stir to mix. Reduce the heat and fry for 2 to 3 minutes.

Serve garnished with the reserved mushrooms, along with the fried eggs, extra parsley, lemon wedges, and avocado slices.

**Tip**
*Serve with a tangy salad.*

**VE** Opt for nutritional yeast; omit the eggs to serve.
**GF** ✓

# hipotle Jackfruit Tacos

MAKES 8 TACOS/SERVES 4 AS A MAIN OR
    8 AS A STARTER

vegetable oil, for frying

2 (14-ounce) cans green (young) jackfruit
    in brine, drained

½ cup plus 2 tablespoons water or
    vegetable stock

SPICE MIX:

2 garlic cloves, minced

1 teaspoon grated fresh ginger or
    ground ginger

2 tablespoons nutritional yeast (optional)

1 tablespoon dried oregano

1 tablespoon chipotle paste

1 teaspoon smoked paprika

1 teaspoon ground cumin

1 teaspoon ground coriander

1 teaspoon ground cinnamon or raw
    cacao powder

¾ teaspoon salt, plus more to taste

¼ teaspoon freshly ground black pepper

2 tablespoons red wine vinegar

2 tablespoons olive oil

TO SERVE:

8 corn tortillas

fresh salad toppings of your choice, such
    as chopped or sliced avocado, red
    onion, peppers, tomatoes, cucumber,
    cabbage, and/or baby spinach lime
    wedges

nutritonal yeast, to sprinkle (optional)

½ cup plus 2 tablespoons dairy or vegan
    sour cream

hot sauce, such as Cholula or other
    hot sauces containing jalapeños or
    habanero chiles (sriracha sauce will
    also do the trick)

**A great taco offers a variety of textures and flavors, and this easy recipe featuring spicy jackfruit ticks all the boxes. The toppings of cilantro, avocado, and sour cream offer a fresh, cool contrast. Many people enjoy tacos frequently, using ready-made spice mixes. Impress your guests by making your own spice mix—it adds a vibrant homemade flavor that is superior to store-bought mixes. These tacos are enhanced with a little kick of chipotle heat—chipotle is a dried and smoky variety of jalapeño. You can substitute another chile for the chipotle paste, if you like.**

Mix together all the ingredients for the spice mix in a bowl, mashing them into a paste. Heat a skillet over medium heat. Add a drizzle of vegetable oil and then the spice mix, breaking it up with a wooden spoon. And the jackfruit and fry, stirring, for 2 to 3 minutes until the pieces are well coated with the spice mix. Add the water and simmer the jackfruit for 20 minutes; if the pan dries out too quickly, add a little more water. Taste and adjust the seasoning with salt, then set aside.

Fill the tortillas with the jackfruit and fresh salad toppings of your choice and serve with lime wedges, nutritional yeast (if desired), sour cream, and hot sauce.

**VE** Opt for vegan sour cream to serve.

**GF** Use corn tortillas.

# Bibimbap Bowls

SERVES 4

KIMCHI (makes 1 pound):
1 pound Chinese cabbage or other sturdy
    cabbage variety, coarsely chopped
2½ tablespoons salt
1 tablespoon gochugaru or other hot chile
    paste or hot sauce

vegetable oil, for frying
4 medium organic eggs
1½ cups cooked rice or quinoa
5¼ ounces fried shiitake mushrooms

SAUCE:
1 tablespoon coconut or brown sugar
1 teaspoon grated fresh ginger
1 teaspoon very minced garlic
2 tablespoons water
2 tablespoons shoyu soy sauce or tamari
1 tablespoon toasted sesame oil

TOPPING OPTIONS:
chopped carrot, cucumber, and radishes
tender greens, such as spinach or bok
    choy
bean sprouts
scallions
sesame seeds

**This rendition of a traditional everyday Korean dish features cooked rice (or quinoa), shiitake mushrooms, and a vibrant array of fresh veggies, all fired up with fermented kimchi. It's easily turned into a festive crowd-pleaser with the addition of eye-catching toppings. The kimchi can be prepared two weeks to a few hours before serving. The longer it sits, the more delicious the fermented flavor develops. You can also buy kimchi from Asian supermarkets or health foods stores. Choose an organic brand if you can.**

First make the kimchi: Put the cabbage in a large bowl. Sprinkle with the salt and let sit at room temperature for a few hours, tossing the cabbage carefully halfway through. Rinse the cabbage in a colander and squeeze out the excess liquid with your hands. Transfer to a clean bowl, add the rest of the kimchi ingredients, and mix well. Set aside at room temperature for 1 hour or up to 24 hours to allow the flavors to develop. Store the kimchi in a sterilized jar in the fridge for up to 2 weeks.

Whisk together all the ingredients for the sauce in a measuring cup. Heat a skillet and add a drizzle of vegetable oil. Fry the eggs and set aside until ready to serve (alternatively, serve raw eggs on the hot rice).

To assemble the bibimbap, put the different elements on the table for guests to compose their own bowls or prepare the bowls by adding a serving of the cooked rice or quinoa, fried shiitake mushrooms, kimchi, and a fried egg, along with some of the freshly prepared veggies and any other topping choices. Drizzle the sauce over the rice or quinoa and egg.

**VE** Omit the eggs.
**GF** Opt for gluten-free tamari.

# Eggplant and Red Pepper Lasagna with Cherry Tomatoes

SERVES 4

2½ cups Marinara Sauce (see page 143)

1 roasted red pepper from a jar, drained

9 ounces ricotta

9 ounces mascarpone

1 garlic clove, minced and mashed into a
   paste with ½ teaspoon salt

1 teaspoon lemon juice

4 medium/small eggplants, thinly sliced

olive oil, for brushing

salt and freshly ground black pepper,
   to taste

1¾ ounces baby spinach or Kale Chips
   (see page 15)

⅓ cup basil

a handful of cherry tomatoes, halved,
   to garnish

**This is what I would call a lady lasagna, as it's got lots of flavor but without the heaviness. That's because it's made with eggplant slices instead of the usual lasagna noodles, which results in a lighter, altogether juicier dish.**

Preheat the oven to 400°F. Put the marinara sauce and roasted red pepper in a blender or food processor and blend until smooth. Mix the ricotta and mascarpone or vegan cream cheese with the garlic and lemon juice in a bowl.

Brush the eggplant slices with olive oil and lightly sprinkle with salt and pepper. Arrange a layer of eggplant slices in the bottom of a baking dish, then cover with a thin layer of the marinara sauce. Add a layer of spinach or kale and add a handful of basil (reserve a few leaves for the top). Repeat the layers, finishing with a final layer of eggplant slices, and top with the ricotta mixture. Arrange the cherry tomato halves and basil leaves on top, press them down into the ricotta mixture, then season lightly with salt and pepper. Bake for 25 minutes, checking 5 minutes before the end of the baking time to ensure that the lasagna isn't burning. Serve hot, with a fresh salad alongside.

### Tip
*The lasagna can be prepared a day ahead, cooled, and kept, covered, in the fridge. Reheat in a preheated 400°F oven for 10 minutes.*

**VE** Opt for vegan cream cheese instead of the
ricotta and mascarpone.

**GF** ✓

# Roasted Ragù and Pappardelle

SERVES 4

olive oil, for drizzling

14 ounces dried pappardelle or pasta
    of your choice

6 tablespoons dry white wine

2½ ounces Parmesan, grated, or
    rawmesan (see page 28), or
    2 tablespoons nutritional yeast

¼ cup black olives, pitted

1 teaspoon honey or agave syrup

salt and freshly ground black pepper,
    to taste

ROASTED RAGÙ:

olive oil, for drizzling

1¾ pounds mushrooms, such as shiitake,
    portobello, or white button,
    coarsely chopped

14 ounces good-quality small tomatoes,
    halved

2 eggplants, trimmed and cut into
    small wedges

1 red bell pepper, cored, seeded, and cut
    into thick strips

6 shallots, cut into wedges

3 garlic cloves, peeled but left whole

salt, for sprinkling

1 tablespoon freshly ground fennel seeds

1 tablespoon chopped fresh rosemary
    leaves or thyme leaves

1 teaspoon red pepper flakes

TO SERVE:

extra-virgin olive oil

basil

grated Parmesan or rawmesan (see
    page 28), or breadcrumbs

**Italian food is naturally full of fresh vegetables and this family-style pasta dish features roasted mushrooms, tomatoes, and eggplant in a scrumptious ragù, although you can easily vary the vegetables according to your taste or what's in season. Pappardelle gives the dish a rustic quality and soaks up the sauce and herbs for a mouth-watering experience.**

To make the roasted ragù, preheat the oven to 400°F. Line a large baking sheet with parchment paper.

Arrange all the prepared vegetables (including the garlic) in a single layer on the lined baking sheet. Drizzle with olive oil and sprinkle with salt and the ground fennel seeds, rosemary, and red pepper flakes. Roast for 45 to 55 minutes, checking frequently during the last 20 minutes of roasting time to make sure the veggies aren't burning.

Meanwhile, bring a large pot of water to a boil and add a drizzle of olive oil and a generous pinch of salt. Cook the pappardelle for 2 minutes less than instructed on the package. Turn off the heat and drain the pasta, reserving 2½ cups of the cooking water. Return the pasta to the pan with the reserved cooking water and add a drizzle of olive oil to keep it moist and give it a sheen.

Pick out the roasted garlic cloves from the baking sheet, crush them with a fork, and mix them into the pasta. Add the roasted veggies, wine, Parmesan or rawmesan or nutritional yeast, olives, and honey or agave syrup and heat over medium-high heat. Simmer briskly, stirring gently, for 2 to 2½ minutes until the liquid has reduced and been absorbed by the pasta. Taste and adjust the seasoning with salt and pepper, drizzle with extra-virgin olive oil, and serve sprinkled with basil and extra Parmesan, rawmesan, or breadcrumbs.

**VE** Use egg-free pasta; opt for rawmesan or nutritional yeast.
**GF** Use gluten-free pasta, and gluten-free breadcrumbs (if using) to serve.

# Roasted Baby Pumpkins Stuffed with Harissa Lentils

SERVES 6

3 baby pumpkins or small squashes
olive oil, for brushing
salt, for sprinkling

STUFFING:

7 ounces dried Puy lentils, rinsed
   and drained
1¾ ounces harissa
2 tablespoons olive oil
½ cup dried white breadcrumbs or
   panko breadcrumbs
4 shallots, diced
3 garlic cloves, minced
a handful of raisins, minced
leaves from 6 thyme sprigs
1 teaspoon ground cumin
juice of ½ lemon
salt and freshly ground black pepper,
   to taste

ZESTY TAHINI CREAM:

3 tablespoons tahini
3 tablespoons olive oil
1 garlic clove
½ teaspoon salt
1 teaspoon honey or agave syrup
2 tablespoons lemon juice

TO SERVE:

mint leaves
a handful of toasted nuts, such as pecans,
   walnuts, or almonds
1¾ ounces feta or goat's cheese,
   crumbled

**When you want to create a showstopping, full-flavored beauty of a dish, go for this one, presented in mini pumpkins or squashes as edible serving bowls. This recipe uses a typical North African flavor palette, combining Puy lentils with spicy harissa, raisins, cumin, feta, and nuts, drizzled with a zesty tahini cream for a decadent and delicious finish.**

Preheat the oven to 375°F. Halve the pumpkins or squashes horizontally. Spoon out the seeds and membranes, then brush the pumpkins or squashes inside and outside with olive oil and sprinkle with salt. Place the pumpkins or squashes on a baking sheet (trim a small slice off the bottoms, if needed, to help stabilize them) and roast for 45 minutes.

To prepare the stuffing, bring 4 cups water to a boil in a saucepan. Add the lentils, reduce the heat, and simmer gently for 20 to 25 minutes until tender. Drain and rinse in cold water; transfer to a bowl. Whisk together the harissa with the olive oil to make a smooth sauce. Add to the cooked lentils and stir. Add all the remaining stuffing ingredients and mix together well.

Divide the lentil stuffing among the pumpkin or squash halves. (The pumpkins can be prepared and stuffed up to a day before serving. Store, covered, in the fridge until ready to cook.) Roast for 20 minutes.

Meanwhile, in a bowl, mix together the ingredients for the tahini cream. It can be made a day ahead, sealed, and stored in the fridge until 20 minutes before serving.

Serve with fresh mint leaves, a few nuts, crumbled feta cheese, and the tahini cream.

**VE** Opt for agave syrup. Use vegan cheese.
**GF** Use gluten-free breadcrumbs.

# Tunisian Eggplant and Pepper Stew with Couscous

SERVES 4

olive oil, for frying

4 shallots, minced

1 red bell pepper, cored, seeded, and
   sliced into strips

2 garlic cloves, minced

2 medium eggplants, chopped

¾ teaspoon salt, plus more to taste

1 (14-ounce) can chopped tomatoes

4 or 5 sun-dried tomatoes in oil, drained
   and minced (optional)

juice of ½ lemon

3 dried figs or other dried fruit,
   minced

400ml vegetable stock

TABIL SPICE MIX:

1½ tablespoons coriander seeds

¾ tablespoon cumin seeds

1½ teaspoons caraway seeds

½ teaspoon red pepper flakes

COUSCOUS:

1¾ cups vegetable stock

1¼ cups whole grain couscous or quinoa

YOGURT DRESSING:

¾ cup Greek or vegan yogurt

a small handful of chopped mint

1 teaspoon honey or agave syrup

salt and freshly ground black pepper,
   to taste

TO SERVE:

a handful of flat-leaf parsley leaves

flatbreads

baby spinach

toasted almonds

orange wedges (optional)

a handful of pomegranate seeds
   (optional)

**Tunisian cooking is often overshadowed by the celebrated Moroccan cuisine, but after being introduced to it, I fell in love! Tunisian food is a blend of Mediterranean and North African flavors, and the characteristic spice mix is tabil, widely used on bread and in various warm dishes, and featured in this eggplant one. Here the eggplant and spices are married together in a tagine-style stew, which is both comforting and exciting, drizzled with a creamy yogurt dressing.**

Heat a skillet over medium heat and toast the tabil spice mix, stirring, for 20 to 30 seconds only. Grind in a spice or coffee grinder, or pulse in a blender, to fine granules. Set aside.

Heat a large saucepan over medium heat. Add a drizzle of olive oil and fry the shallots and bell pepper, stirring frequently, for 5 to 7 minutes until translucent. Add the garlic, eggplant, and tabil spice mix and a drizzle of olive oil, then stir to coat the eggplant with the spice mix. Fry for about 5 minutes until the eggplant is nicely browned. Add the salt, tomatoes, lemon juice, dried figs or other dried fruit, and stock, mix together well, and simmer for 15 minutes while you make the couscous and the yogurt dressing.

For the couscous, bring the vegetable stock to a boil. Put the couscous (or quinoa) in a bowl. Pour over the boiling stock and let soak for 10 minutes.

Mix together all the ingredients for the yogurt dressing in a bowl.

Taste and adjust the seasoning of the eggplant stew with salt, then serve with the couscous (or quinoa), flatbreads, spinach, and almonds, as well as orange wedges and pomegranate seeds, if desired.

**VE** Opt for vegan yogurt.

**GF** Opt for quinoa instead of couscous and use gluten-free flatbreads.

# 6. SIDES AND SHARING DISHES

Side dishes sometimes turn out to be the most exciting component of a meal. So for this chapter I've gathered together some of my all-time favorites that work just as well served as sharing dishes as they do in support of mains. On offer is a mix of those that provide a counterbalance or calming, cooling backdrop to feistier dishes and others that add a powerful injection of concentrated flavor.

It's easy to put together a selection of these dishes to make a great sharing table, from which your guests can mix and match to create an exciting, varied meal, or combine them with dishes from elsewhere in the book. You can also simply serve them as accompaniments to lead dishes, or on their own as starters.

# Crispy Sesame Broccoli

SERVES 8

2½ cups panko breadcrumbs

grated zest of ½ orange

1 teaspoon red pepper flakes

½ teaspoon salt

olive oil, for drizzling

2¼ pounds broccoli, cut down the length with the florets

2 tablespoons tahini

2 tablespoons shoyu soy sauce or tamari

1 garlic clove, peeled and crushed

**A quick roasting of these broccoli stems gives them a pleasing crunchy bite, and then they are coated in nutty tahini and panko breadcrumbs for extra deliciousness. This works perfectly when contrasted with smooth-textured dishes, such as Tofu Dengaku (see page 125) or Lemongrass and Butternut Squash Soup (see page 139).**

Preheat the oven to 425°F. Line a baking sheet with parchment paper.

Mix together the panko, orange zest, red pepper flakes, and salt. Heat a skillet over medium heat. Add a little drizzle of olive oil and fry the panko mixture, stirring, for 3 to 4 minutes until golden. Transfer to a bowl and set aside.

Toss the broccoli with about 1 tablespoon olive oil in a bowl, then arrange in a single layer, without overlapping, on the lined baking sheet. Roast for 8 minutes, then flip the broccoli over and roast for an additional 7 minutes. While the broccoli is roasting, mix together the tahini, soy, and garlic.

Remove the broccoli from the oven and dip one side of each stalk in the tahini mixture and then in the panko mixture. Place on a platter and sprinkle with the rest of the panko mixture. Serve hot.

VE ✓

**GF** Use gluten-free breadcrumbs instead of panko; opt for tamari sauce.

*Left to right
from top:
Sambal Goreng
Buncis, page 126,
Lemongrass and
Butternut Squash
Soup, page 139,
Jackfruit Bulgogi,
page 125, Jackfruit
Bulgogi Salad,
page 89, Tofu
Dengaku,
page 125.*

# Jackfruit Bulgogi

The Jacktree bears the biggest fruit in the world and its stringy fleshy texture makes it ideal to use as a savory addition to salads, breads, and stews, This delicious jackfruit bulgogi can be added to salads, like the Asian-style one on page 89. I use canned green jackfruit in brine, which you will easily find in Asian supermarkets or online. It's important that you choose green jackfruit, as ripe jackfruit is sweet and is best used in dessert.

———

SERVES 4

1½ (14-ounce) cans green jackfruit, drained
vegetable oil, for frying
water as needed
sesame seeds

MARINADE:

1 tablespoon olive oil
3 tablespoons shoyu soy sauce or tamari
¾ tablespoon gochujang chile paste or sriracha
1 teaspoon freshly grated ginger
1 garlic clove, crushed
1 tablespoon coconut sugar or agave syrup
1 tablespoon toasted sesame oil
1 teaspoon lemon juice
salt and freshly ground black pepper, to taste

Put the jackfruit in a bowl. Mix the marinade ingredients together and pour over the jackfruit. Massage the jackfruit with your hands, breaking up the bigger pieces and working the marinade into the fruit. Let marinate for 10 minutes (or up to 24 hours in the fridge), if desired, or fry right away.

Heat a pan over medium-high heat, add a drizzle of oil, and fry the jackfruit. Add a little water to ensure the jackfruit doesn't dry out too quickly. Continue frying and adding small amounts of water for 15 minutes. Fry for an additional 5 minutes without adding water to let the jackfruit dry out. Taste and adjust the seasoning with salt and pepper. This is delicious served warm, sprinkled with sesame seeds, but can also be served cold.

VE ✓

GF Opt for gluten-free tamari.

# Tofu Dengaku

Not everyone loves tofu, but if you're among those who do, this traditional Japanese recipe is simply irresistible. Tofu is brushed with a miso-based glaze to give its neutral taste a serious boost of flavor and finished under intense dry heat to make it deliciously crisp on the outside.

———

SERVES 6

1 (16-ounce) block firm tofu, drained
½ teaspoon sesame seeds
1 scallion, minced

MISO GLAZE:

¼ cup red miso paste or other miso of your choice
1 tablespoon shoyu soy sauce or tamari
1 tablespoon agave syrup
1½ tablespoons mirin
1½ tablespoons sake
1 tablespoon rice vinegar
1 tablespoon grated fresh ginger

Preheat the broiler to high or preheat the oven to 465°F. Line a baking sheet with parchment paper.

Lightly press the tofu between sheets of paper towel and leave for a few minutes to absorb the excess moisture. Meanwhile, mix together all the ingredients for the miso glaze in a bowl until smooth.

Slice the tofu into equal bite-size pieces. Heat a skillet over high heat and fry the tofu for about 2 minutes on each side until golden brown. Transfer the tofu pieces to the lined baking sheet and brush the miso glaze generously over the top of each. Broil for 3½ to 4 minutes until dark brown. If your oven doesn't have a fan function, prop the door open slightly to ensure that the tofu doesn't steam in its own moisture.

Transfer the tofu to a plate, insert a cocktail skewer into each piece, and sprinkle with the sesame seeds and scallion. It's best served warm, but can be enjoyed after cooling down. The miso glaze can be prepared a day in advance and kept, tightly covered or in an airtight container, in the fridge.

VE ✓

GF Choose a gluten-free miso paste and opt for gluten-free tamari.

# Sambal Goreng Buncis

**Sambal goreng buncis is a popular Indonesian dish and one of my favorite ways to eat green beans, cooked with coconut milk, chile, ginger, and garlic. This dish is lovely served with rice, grilled vegetables, eggs, tofu, or pickles.**

SERVES 4

vegetable oil, for frying

14 ounces green beans, cut into about 2-inch lengths

1 cup coconut milk

2 to 3 kaffir lime leaves (optional)

SPICE PASTE:

4 garlic cloves, crushed

1 shallot or small red onion, chopped

1 lemongrass stalk, tough outer layers and stalk top removed, bulb end trimmed and sliced (use only the purple-tinged rings)

1 tablespoon minced fresh ginger

1 tablespoon ground or minced fresh galangal

2 tablespoons vegetable oil

2 tablespoons shoyu soy sauce or tamari

1 tablespoon coconut sugar

1 tablespoon fresh lime juice

1 to 3 teaspoons sambal oelek or other hot chile sauce, such as sriracha, or minced fresh red chile, to taste

½ teaspoon salt, plus extra to taste

Put all the ingredients for the spice paste in a blender and blend to a smooth paste.

Heat a large skillet over medium heat. Add a drizzle of vegetable oil and fry the spice paste, stirring, for 1 to 2 minutes until it starts to dry out. Add the beans and stir-fry until they are thoroughly covered with the spice paste. Add the coconut milk and bring to a boil, then reduce the heat to a simmer. Add the kaffir lime leaves, if using, and cook the beans for about 15 minutes or until they are tender but still have some bite—the exact cooking time will depend on the type and thickness of the beans, but it's usually 10 to 20 minutes. Remove the kaffir lime leaves. Taste and adjust the seasoning with salt. Serve warm.

**VE** ✓ **GF** Opt for gluten-free tamari.

# Seared Miso Mushrooms

**Flavored with miso, these mushrooms are pure umami bombs, adding a powerful flavor hit wherever they are used and making any vegetarian dish truly mouth-watering. I've chosen oyster mushrooms here, which are more delicate than the fleshy shiitakes.**

SERVES 4

2 tablespoons red miso paste (aka miso)

2 tablespoons ghee, butter or vegetable oil, plus extra for frying

9 ounces oyster mushrooms

Mix the miso with the ghee, butter or oil until smooth. Heat a skillet over high heat. Add a little ghee, butter or oil and fry the mushrooms for 2 minutes without stirring, then fry for an additional 2 minutes while stirring. Add the miso and fry, stirring, for a final minute. Serve warm as a side.

**VE** Opt for vegetable oil.

**GF** Use a dark miso paste instead of red but check the contents to ensure that it's gluten-free.

# Tsukemono

Historically, pickling was used as a way of preserving vegetables and fruit for the winter. Although it's still a useful method for extending the shelf life of foods, the major win with pickling is the amazing flavors that result. Pickles add interest and finish to dishes, but there is much more to pickles than the little kosher dills or gherkins we are used to, in particular tsukemono, the prince of pickles. Delicately flavored, these Japanese pickles provide a striking contrast to fresh, light food such as steamed dishes and cooked rice.

Use this brine to pickle any fresh vegetables you like, and serve them in stews, salads, or breads or to top canapés.

---

MAKES 1 POUND PICKLES
1 pound vegetables of your choice, such as
    cucumber, shallots, zucchini, turnips, radishes,
    and/or carrots, peeled as appropriate and thinly
    sliced or cut into matchsticks

BRINE:
1 cup umeboshi vinegar or shoyu soy sauce or tamari
1 cup rice vinegar

OPTIONAL BRINE ADD-INS:
a small amount of wasabi
thinly sliced ginger
red shiso seasoning

Mix the ingredients for the brine together, including any add-ins, in a glass measuring cup. Put the prepared veggies in one large or two smaller sterilized jars. Pour over the brine to cover and seal the jar(s). Let pickle in the fridge for 3 days before serving. Once opened, use the pickles within 3 to 4 days. The pickles will keep, unopened, in the fridge for up to 2 weeks, if a sterile jar is used.

VE ✓
GF Opt for gluten-free tamari.

## Tip
*Umeboshi vinegar colors the veggies less than either soy sauce and tamari, so for brighter-colored pickles, opt for that.*

# Wakame Salad

If you are looking for an easy way to enjoy sea vegetables, look no further. In fact, I recommend that you flag this page in the book because this recipe is phenomenal in so many ways. As well as serving it as a salad, you can add it to Asian rice bowls and soups, serve it with eggs and avocados, or use it as a sandwich filling with fresh potatoes and egg salad or topping. It's also great served as a side with Scandinavian-style dishes, as Japanese and Nordic flavors marry perfectly.

---

SERVES 4
1 ounce dried wakame

DRESSING:
2 tablespoons rice vinegar
2 tablespoons light soy sauce or tamari
2 teaspoons sesame seeds
1 teaspoon shichimi togarashi or red pepper flakes,
    or more to taste
1 teaspoon sugar

Soak the wakame in a bowl of warm water for 10 to 20 minutes. Meanwhile, bring a saucepan of water to a boil. Drain the wakame and blanch in the boiling water for 30 seconds. Immediately drain in a sieve and rinse with very cold water. Drain thoroughly and pat with a clean dish towel to absorb the excess moisture. Chop the wakame and transfer to a serving bowl.

Mix together all the ingredients for the dressing in a small bowl, pour over the wakame, and serve.

The salad can be kept, tightly covered or in an airtight container, in the fridge for 2 to 3 days.

VE ✓
GF Opt for gluten-free tamari.

# Baby Bok Choy with Ginger and Garlic

Bok choy is one of my best-loved cabbages! Smooth and crunchy at the same time, it's simply delicious and so easy to cook. There is very little fuss involved in preparing this dish—it's the quality of the ingredients that makes all the difference. This goes well with the Seared Miso Mushrooms (see page 126) and rice dishes.

SERVES 4

4 head baby bok choy
1 tablespoon sesame oil
1 garlic clove, crushed
1 teaspoon grated fresh ginger
2 tablespoons shoyu soy sauce or tamari
5 tablespoons water
2 tablespoons sesame seeds

Cut the bok choy lengthwise into wedges, keeping the root intact so that the leaves stay together.

Heat a large deep skillet or wok that has a lid over medium-high heat. Add the sesame oil, garlic, ginger, and soy sauce or tamari and stir briefly to combine. Add the water and bok choy, cover the pan with the lid, and steam for 2 minutes.

Remove from the heat and sprinkle with the sesame seeds. Serve warm.

VE ✓
GF Opt for gluten-free tamari.

# Cherry Chutney and Radicchio with Toasted Almonds

Chutney is a smart shortcut to maximizing flavor, great for using with quality salad and other vegetables to create standout dishes. Here a few spoonfuls of concentrated chutney are enough to transform radicchio leaves into a scrumptious warm salad. This is ideal for serving as a side dish with curries.

You can use other fruit or berries or vegetables in place of cherries for the chutney.

To make the chutney, heat a skillet over medium-high heat. Add a drizzle of olive oil or a little ghee and fry the shallots, ginger, garlic, chile, spices, fennel seeds, and seasoning with the sugar, stirring frequently, for 5 to 7 minutes or until the shallots are translucent. Add the cherries and red vinegar, reduce the heat, cover, and leave the chutney to simmer for 25 to 30 minutes, stirring occasionally, until the liquid has reduced and the consistency is thick.

Transfer the chutney to a sterilized airtight jar and let cool. Seal the jar and store in the fridge for up to 2 weeks, until ready to use.

To prepare the salad, heat a skillet over medium heat. Add a drizzle of vegetable oil and then the chutney, breaking it up with a wooden spoon. Add the radicchio and fry for 2 to 3 minutes, stirring and tossing the leaves to coat with the chutney. Taste and adjust the seasoning with salt and pepper. Sprinkle with toasted almonds and serve.

**VE** Opt for olive oil.
**GF** ✓

---

**Tip**
*Make this a filling main salad dish by adding delicate green salad leaves, avocado, sautéed mushrooms, and cooked grains. Dilute the chutney with olive oil and vinegar or lemon juice to use as a dressing.*

CHERRY CHUTNEY (MAKES 12 TO 14 OUNCES):

olive oil or ghee, for frying
4 shallots, thinly sliced
2 teaspoons freshly grated ginger
2 garlic cloves, crushed
1 red chile, seeded and minced
1 teaspoon ground cardamom
1 teaspoon ground cinnamon
½ teaspoon fennel seeds
¼ teaspoon freshly ground
   black pepper
salt, to taste
2 tablespoons coconut sugar or
   brown sugar
7 ounces pitted cherries
6 tablespoons red wine vinegar

CHERRY CHUTNEY RADICCHIO
   SALAD:
vegetable oil, for frying
2 to 3 tablespoons Cherry
   Chutney (see left)
5 ounces radicchio leaves (or
   other sturdy salad leaves), torn
   into pieces
salt and freshly ground black
   pepper, to taste
toasted almonds (or other
   nuts), coarsely chopped, for
   sprinkling

# Labneh and Harissa-Roasted Carrots with Mint and Almonds

SERVES 4

LABNEH:

2 cups full-fat Greek yogurt

½ cup plus 2 tablespoons good-quality
    extra-virgin olive oil

a handful of mixed herbs, such as mint,
    flat-leaf parsley, and chives

1 teaspoon finely grated lemon zest

salt and freshly ground black pepper,
    to taste

HARISSA ROASTED CARROTS:

14 ounces baby carrots or carrots,
    halved lengthwise

6 tablespoons olive oil

2 tablespoons harissa

salt, to taste

TO SERVE:

crumbled toasted almonds

fresh mint leaves

extra-virgin olive oil

salt and freshly ground black pepper,
    to taste

sprinkles of sumac (optional)

**Contrasting flavors make powerful combinations. In this sharing dish, harissa, a chile paste full of slow-roasted hot pepper flavor, spices up humble carrots, paired against a cool labneh. It's easy to make your own labneh, a soft cheese made from strained yogurt. It needs at least a few days in the fridge before it's ready; you can use shop-bought labneh instead if time is in short supply. It's available from Middle Eastern supermarkets and many well-stocked Western supermarkets and delis.**

To make the labneh, line a sieve with cheesecloth and place over a large bowl. Put the yogurt in the cheesecloth, then gather up the cloth edges and twist together. Put the yogurt in the fridge and let drain for 3 days.

Discard the liquid in the bowl. Shape the yogurt, which will have thickened into a fresh cheese, into balls and place in a deep bowl or sterilized jar. Mix together the extra-virgin olive oil, herbs, lemon zest, and salt and pepper to taste and pour the mixture over the labneh. Cover the bowl tightly or seal the jar and leave the labneh to marinate in the fridge for 1 day or up to 1 week.

To make the harissa-roasted carrots, preheat the oven to 400°F. Line a baking sheet with parchment paper. Mix together the olive oil and harissa in a bowl. Add the carrots and salt to taste and toss to coat with the harissa mixture. Spread the carrots on the lined baking sheet and roast for 40 minutes, keeping an eye on the baking sheet for the last 10 minutes to avoid burning.

To serve, spread the labneh on a plate and top the labneh with the harissa-roasted carrots, toasted almonds, and fresh mint leaves. Drizzle with extra-virgin olive oil, and sprinkle with salt, pepper, and sumac, if using.

**VE** Opt for vegan soft cheese and use olive oil for frying.

**GF** ✓

### Tip

*Labneh is often served with hummus (see page 34). It can also be whipped and used as as tangy butter cream on cakes (see Chai Carrot Cake on page 186, just omit the herbs and add 2 teaspoons honey or agave syrup) or served plain, drizzled with honey or syrup and sprinkled with typical Middle Eastern toppings such as nuts, pomegranate seeds, warming spices such as cinnamon or cardamom, or with preserved or fresh fruit.*

# The Big Roast!

SERVES 8

1 medium butternut squash, halved
    lengthwise, seeded, peeled, and sliced
    into wedges
6 beets, peeled and cut into wedges
2 red bell peppers, cored, seeded and cut
    into thick strips
12 carrots, cut into
    chunky pieces
4 red onions, cut into wedges
extra virgin olive oil, for drizzling
5 sage leaves, finely chopped
leaves from 4 thyme sprigs
salt, to taste
sprinkling of red pepper flakes, to taste
6 tablespoons toasted pumpkin seeds

YOGURT LEMON GARLIC SAUCE:

¾ cup yogurt or coconut yogurt
1 teaspoon lemon juice
1 garlic clove, crushed to a paste with
    ¾ teaspoon salt
1 teaspoon honey or agave syrup

**I made this huge roast for my beloved family for one of the first dinners I hosted in my home. I wanted to make a vegetarian meal that they would all love, and this great big colorful sheet of roasted veggies did the job perfectly. It's a very easy recipe where butternut squash, beet, carrots, peppers, and onions are roasted together with sage and thyme, then drizzled with a cool lemon-flavored yogurt sauce. Serve with couscous, any grain, or fresh bread.**

Preheat the oven to 425°F. Line two large baking sheets with parchment paper. Mix together all the ingredients for the yogurt lemon garlic sauce in a bowl and set aside until ready to serve.

Put the prepared veggies in a large bowl, drizzle with olive oil, sprinkle with the herbs, and season to taste with the salt and red pepper flakes. Toss to coat and then arrange the vegetables in a single layer, without overlapping, on the lined baking sheets. Roast for 45 minutes or until the veggies are tender. Serve the roasted veggies hot, sprinkled with toasted pumpkin seeds and with the yogurt sauce alongside.

Tip
*The roast can be varied with the seasons, using other root vegetables and/or different squashes in the recipe.*

VE Use vegan yogurt; opt for agave.
GF ✓

From top left:
*Best Tomato Salad Ever, page 138. Roasted Parsnip Fries with Ajvar Dip, page 138. Hurricane Popcorn, page 12. Kimchi Fried Rice, page 139. Furikake, page 166. Potatoes Seruendeng, page 138. Rainbow Noodles with Cilantro Pesto, page 139.*

# Potatoes Serundeng

Serundeng is a seasoning of spice-tempered coconut flakes often used to liven up rice and curries in Indonesia. It's utterly delicious. I use serundeng on a variety of foods, and here I'm transforming potatoes with it. Serve with curries or a fresh salad. Try sprinkling serundeng on roasted vegetables or root veggies.

SERVES 4
1¾ pounds quality firm potatoes
salt, to taste
vegetable oil or butter

SERUNDENG (MAKES ABOUT 1 POUND):
1 pound dessicated coconut
½ cup coconut sugar
1 teaspoon ground cumin
3 garlic cloves, crushed
1 teaspoon fresh fresh ginger
1 teaspoon ground coriander
½ teaspoon salt
1½ cups roasted peanuts, crushed

Boil the potatoes for 15 to 20 minutes, checking for doneness after 15 minutes, until the potatoes are soft. Drain and set aside.

Meanwhile, make the serundeng. Heat a skillet over medium-high heat. Fry the coconut while continously stirring until the coconut is a deep golden color, 2 to 3 minutes. Add the sugar, spices, and salt and continue stirring to mix well. Add the peanuts and stir, then remove from the heat. Toss the potatoes with oil or butter and sprinkle generously with serundeng. Serve warm.

**Tip**
*Keep any leftover serundeng stored, sealed, in a cool place.*

VE ✓ GF ✓

# Roasted Parsnip Fries with Ajvar Dip

Parsnip is one of the more underrated root vegetables, and it deserves more attention. Its best flavor comes out when roasted. Use as a side dish, where you normally would use potatoes, sweet potatoes, or rice. Here I paired it with a Hungarian red pepper dip, ajvar. It's a delicious dip that can be used with breads, salads, and pizzas too.

SERVES 4
AJVAR DIP:
1 eggplant, halved
4 red bell peppers, cut into pieces
5 garlic cloves
3 tablespoons olive oil
1 teaspoon lemon juice
1 teaspoon agave syrup or honey
salt and pepper, to taste

6 parsnips, cut into strips or wedges
olive oil
1 tablespoon rosemary or thyme (chopped fresh or dried)
salt

Preheat the oven to 425°F. Line a baking sheet with parchment paper. To make the ajvar dip: Place the eggplant, bell peppers, and garlic on a baking sheet and roast for 10 minutes. Remove the garlic and roast the eggplant and peppers for another 30 minutes. Let cool, transfer to a food processor, and add the rest of the ajvar ingredients. Process until well combined. Taste and adjust the seasoning with salt and pepper. Toss the parsnip with the herbs and oil in a bowl and spread out in a single layer on the lined baking sheet. Roast for 25 to 30 minutes. Serve warm as a side or as a small bite with another dip (like the artichoke dip on page 34).

VE Opt for agave syrup. GF ✓

# Best Tomato Salad Ever

Tomato salads work wonders as a side with savory dishes. But there's a well-known secret that makes all the difference between a bland tomato salad and a magnificent one. If you marinate the tomatoes in a sour liquid (lemon juice in the summer and vinegar in the winter), garlic, salt, and a sweetener (if you are using balsamic vingar use less) you get the most wonderful and delicious tomato salad. Serve it just as it is or include as many add-ons as you like.

SERVES 4
14 ounces quality tomatoes, chopped or sliced
6 tablespoons vinegar or lemon juice
2 garlic cloves, crushed to a paste with ¾ teaspoon salt
2 teaspoons honey or agave syrup
6 tablespoons extra-virgin olive oil

OPTIONAL ADD-ONS
1 red onion, minced or thinly sliced
fresh green leaves such as baby spinach or arugula
fresh herbs, such as basil or parsley
mozzarella or feta cheese or vegan cheese

Mix the tomato and the marinade ingredients in a bowl, taste, and adjust the flavor with salt or sweetener. Let marinate for 30 minutes to 2 hours. You can choose to drain the liquid from the bowl or keep it in the salad as a dressing. Add add-ons as you like for a fuller salad.

VE Opt for vegan cheese and agave syrup.
GF ✓

# Kimchi Fried Rice

Rice can easily become the main attraction on the table; just fry it with kimchi and it will be both exciting and hot! Try the kimchi on page 109, or use store-bought kimchi, but make sure it's good quality.

—

SERVES 4

3 tablespoons kimchi (see page 109)
2 tablespoons shoyu soy sauce or tamari
sesame oil or other vegetable oil, for frying
3 cups cooked brown rice
a handful of fresh herbs like cilantro or parsley, or baby spinach

Blend the kimchi with the soy sauce and 1 tablespoon sesame oil. In a bowl, mix the rice and the kimchi mixture.

Heat a pan over medium-high heat, add the rice, and cook for 4 minutes. Taste and adjust the flavor, adding kimchi brine or soy sauce if needed. Lower the temperature and cook the rice, stirring, for an additional 2 minutes. Serve warm, mixed with fresh herbs.

**VE** ✓
**GF** Opt for gluten-free tamari.

# Rainbow Noodles with Cilantro Pesto

This is an incredibly juicy and fresh option for noodles, pasta, and rice. Spiralize rainbow carrots, zucchini, daikon radish, and other suitable vegetables and serve with a pesto made of cilantro, lime, garlic, ginger, sesame oil, and chile.

—

SERVES 4

CILANTRO PESTO:
1 cup fresh cilantro
6 tablespoons olive oil, and extra to taste
2 tablespoons toasted sesame oil
5 tablespoons roasted cashews or other nuts
juice of 1 lime, or 2 tablespoons lemon juice
1 tablespoon nutritional yeast or finely grated Parmesan (optional)
salt, to taste

1¾ pounds vegetables, such as rainbow carrots, zucchini, or daikon radish, peeled and spiralized

Blend the pesto ingredients into a smooth paste. Add a little extra water if you want a looser consistency.

Serve the pesto with spiralized veggies or use as a condiment with savory dishes.

**VE** Opt for nutritional yeast.
**GF** Opt for gluten-free tamari.

# Lemongrass and Butternut Squash Soup

This warming and vibrant soup balances comforting butternut with lively lemongrass and chile. Serve with fresh salads or rice dishes.

—

SERVES 4

2 butternut squash, halved lengthwise and seeded
olive oil
salt
4 shallots, coarsely chopped
2 garlic cloves, crushed
1⅔ cups vegetable stock
1⅔ cups coconut milk
2 tablespoons pureed lemongrass
1½ teaspoons gochujang, sriracha, or other red chile paste, plus more to taste
1 teaspoon grated fresh ginger
¾ teaspoon salt

Preheat the oven to 425°F. Brush the butternut squash with oil and sprinkle with salt. Roast in the middle of the oven, cut-side up, for 1 hour. Scoop out the flesh and transfer the flesh with the shallots and garlic to a food processor. Blend into a smooth puree.

Add the puree to a saucepan, along with the rest of the soup ingredients. Bring to a boil and lower the heat. Allow to simmer for 2 to 3 minutes. Taste and adjust with salt, if needed

**VE** ✓
**GF** ✓

# 7. AL FRESCO

You can serve many of the dishes in this book outdoors or take them to
potluck gatherings, but the ones in this chapter are extra delicious enjoyed in the open air
or are particularly portable for bringing with you to a barbecue or on a picnic. One popular
choice for a fun and flexible al fresco cooking and dining experience is pizza, and here are lots of
exciting ideas for topping combinations, together with a recipe for a delicious cauliflower
crust as a gluten-free alternative to a spelt and wheat flour dough base.
There is something irresistible about grilling food and eating it outside, so I've
included options for barbecue parties, such as crowd-pleasing Mediterranean-style halloumi
and vegetable skewers complete with grilled pita breads and a creamy red pepper sauce.
But nothing could be more perfect for a bring-your-own get-together than
a beautiful layered green crêpe cake.

*Tahini and Sweet Potato
and Avocado Pizza
page 144.*

——

**Tip**

*It's no problem if you don't have access to an outdoor
pizza oven, as you can cook the pizzas on a hot charcoal or gas grill, or of course pop them into a regular
kitchen oven.*

# Bake-Your-Own Pizza Party

MAKES 4 MEDIUM OR 8 SMALL PIZZAS
OR FLATBREADS

BASIC SPELT DOUGH

4 teaspoons fast-action dried yeast

1¼ cups plus 1 tablespoon warm (not hot)
   water

2 tablespoons honey or agave syrup

4½ cups whole wheat spelt flour, plus
   extra for dusting

3¼ cups all-purpose flour or spelt flour

4 teaspoons fine salt

1 cup olive oil, plus extra for oiling

semolina flour, for dusting the lined
   baking sheet (optional)

MARINARA SAUCE
   (MAKES 3½ CUPS):

olive oil, for frying

2 shallots, chopped

3 garlic cloves, crushed to a paste with 1
   teaspoon fine salt

2 (14-ounce) cans good-quality plum
   tomatoes

a handful of basil, chopped

2 tablespoons mixed dried Italian herbs,
   such as oregano, basil, and thyme
   (optional)

1 teaspoon honey or agave syrup, or more
   to taste

salt and freshly ground black pepper,
   to taste

CLASSIC TOPPINGS:

Marinara sauce, mozzarella, garlic, herbs,
   salt, and freshly ground black pepper

SUGGESTED TOPPING OPTIONS:

peppers, zucchini, eggplant, kale,
   spinach, onions, olives, mushrooms,
   fennel, broccoli, sweet potato, nuts
   and seeds, pesto

VE Opt for agave syrup for the spelt dough and
marinara; opt for vegan alternatives to dairy such as
vegan cheese for the topping.

GF The dough is not gluten-free.

For a family gathering, this pizza-party formula works like a charm. We have a wood-fired stone pizza oven in the corner of the garden, so pizza has become an outdoor meal for us, and the smell of burnt wood and freshly baked pizzas in the fresh air is heavenly. The key concept here is for your guests to simply create their own pizzas, with a portion of the dough that you have prepared in advance (kids will love it especially!), choosing from a variety of toppings that you provide. The thin spelt crust is delicious, and the dough can also be used to make flatbreads.

———

To make the spelt dough, mix the yeast with the warm water and honey or agave syrup in a small bowl. Let stand for about 10 minutes to allow the yeast to activate—it should become foamy on the surface.

Put the flours in a mixing bowl, or in the bowl of a stand mixer fitted with the dough hook, sift over the salt, and mix together well. If mixing by hand, make a well in the flour, pour in the yeast mixture, and gradually mix in the flour with a fork, then slowly add the olive oil and work it into the dough with your hands. Knead the dough on a floured work surface for a few minutes until smooth and elastic. If using a stand mixer, add the yeast mixture with the motor running until incorporated, then slowly pour in the olive oil and continue kneading until the dough is smooth.

Oil a large bowl, add the dough, and cover with a clean dish towel. Set aside to rise in a warm spot for 1½ hours. Punch the dough down to deflate it and place it on a floured work surface. Divide the dough into four or eight pieces and knead each piece lightly into a ball.

To make the marinara, heat a skillet over medium heat. Add a drizzle of olive oil and fry the shallots with the garlic, stirring, for 7 to 8 minutes until soft. Add all the remaining ingredients and simmer for 15 minutes, stirring occasionally to avoid burning. Add a little water or stock if the sauce dries out too much. Taste and adjust the flavor balance with salt, pepper, and honey or agave syrup.

To make the pizzas, lay a sheet of parchment paper on a baking sheet and sprinkle with a little semolina flour—this is optional, but it adds a delicious texture. Roll out one dough ball with a rolling pin into a thin round—it should be only ⅛ inch thick. Add your choice of toppings and transfer to the prepared baking sheet. Repeat with the remaining dough balls.

Baking times vary between different methods and ovens: if using an indoor oven, preheat to 425°F and bake for 10 to 18 minutes until the pizza crust and toppings are golden and well done. If using a grill, place the pizza on the lined baking sheet on the grill grate over the fire and bake until it is well done—the time will vary depending on the heat of your grill. If using a wood-fired stone pizza oven, start a fire in the oven 2 hours ahead of baking, keep adding wood to build up the heat, and loosely close with a lid. Bake the pizza for 1 to 3 minutes. On pages 144 and 146 are some suggestions for toppings.

# Goat's Cheese and Beet Pizza

MAKES 1 PIZZA

¼ quantity Basic Spelt Dough
(see page 143)
olive oil, for drizzling
leaves from 2 sprigs of thyme
3½ ounces soft goat's cheese or vegan
cheese, crumbled
½ medium beet, cooked or raw, peeled
and thinly sliced
1 tablespoon thinly sliced raw red onion
salt and freshly ground black pepper,
to taste

Roll out the dough into a thin round
following the instructions on page 143.
Drizzle with olive oil and sprinkle with
salt and pepper to taste and the thyme.
Top with the goat's cheese or vegan
cheese and then the remaining toppings.
Bake following the instructions on
page 143.

VE Opt for vegan soft cheese.
GF The dough is not gluten-free.

# Kale and Mushroom Pizza

MAKES 1 PIZZA

¼ quantity Basic Spelt Dough (see
page 143)
olive oil, for drizzling
a sprinkle of chopped marjoram
a handful of kale leaves (stalks removed),
chopped
1 garlic clove, crushed
5¼ ounces burrata, sliced or torn, or
vegan soft cheese
a handful of sliced mushrooms
red pepper flakes, for sprinkling
grated Parmesan or rawmesan
(see page 28), for sprinkling
salt and freshly ground black pepper,
to taste

Roll out the dough into a thin round
following the instructions on page 143.
Drizzle with olive oil and sprinkle with salt
and pepper and marjoram.
Put the kale in a bowl with the garlic and
a drizzle of olive oil and massage together
with your hands.
Top the pizza with the burrata or vegan
cheese and the kale, add the mushroom
slices, and sprinkle with red pepper flakes.
Bake following the instructions on page
143, then sprinkle with Parmesan or
rawmesan and salt before serving.

VE Opt for vegan cheese.
GF The dough is not gluten-free.

# Tahini, Sweet Potato, and Avocado Pizza

MAKES 1 PIZZA

¼ quantity Basic Spelt Dough
(see page 143)
olive oil, for drizzling
pinch of red pepper flakes
3 to 4 tablespoons Marinara Sauce (see
page 143)
1 roasted red pepper from a jar, drained
or fresh red pepper, sliced
a handful of fresh spinach
1¾ ounces sweet potato wedges,
precooked
1 tablespoon pine nuts or other nuts
½ avocado, sliced
salt and freshly ground black pepper

TAHINI SAUCE:
2 tablespoons tahini
1 garlic clove, crushed
3 tablespoons fresh cilantro, chopped
6 tablespoons water
3 tablespoons olive oil
3 tablespoons lemon juice
1 teaspoon honey or agave syrup
salt, to taste

Roll out the dough into a thin round
following the instructions on page 143.
Drizzle with olive oil and sprinkle with salt
and pepper and the red pepper flakes.
Put the marinara and roasted red
pepper in a blender or food processor and
blend until smooth—this is delicious with
the tahini. Spread on top of the pizza crust,
add the spinach and sweet potato wedges,
and sprinkle over the pine nuts. Bake
following the instructions on page 143.
Meanwhile, blend together all the
ingredients for the tahini sauce in a pitcher
until well combined.
Top the baked pizza with the avocado
slices and drizzle over the tahini sauce
before serving.

VE Opt for agave syrup for the sauce.
GF The dough is not gluten-free.

# Broccoli and Pesto Pizza

**MAKES 1 PIZZA**

¼ quantity Basic Spelt Dough
  (see page 143)
olive oil, for drizzling
salt and freshly ground black pepper,
  to taste
pinch of red pepper flakes
2 tablespoons pesto
½ garlic clove, crushed
a handful of broccoli rabe or broccoli,
  chopped
2½ ounces mozzarella, torn or sliced, or
  vegan cheese

———

Roll out the dough into a thin round following the instructions on page 143. Drizzle with olive oil and sprinkle with salt and pepper and the red pepper flakes. Spread the pizza crust with the pesto and garlic, then top with the broccoli rabe or broccoli and mozzarella or vegan cheese. Bake following the instructions on page 143.

## Tip

*You can replace the broccoli rabe or broccoli with asparagus, green beans, or other green vegetables.*

**VE** Opt for vegan cheese and use vegan pesto.
**GF** The dough is not gluten-free.

# Salad in a Jar

———

**Packing your salad in a jar isn't just a brilliant lunch option—it's also a delicious, portable solution when you are asked to bring your own food to a party. This jar is layered with cooked grains, tahini sauce, yogurt, grilled vegetables, fresh salad vegetables and herbs, plant protein in the form of chickpeas, and some seeds and nuts for a pleasing crunch.**

———

**SERVES 1**

5½ ounces mixed vegetables, such as
  red bell pepper, cored and seeded,
  and eggplant and zucchini, chopped
olive oil, for grilling
1 tablespoon harissa
salt, to taste
extra-virgin olive oil, for drizzling
1 tablespoon lemon juice
6 tablespoons cooked freekeh, bulgur
  wheat, couscous, or brown rice
6 tablespoons Tahini Sauce (see
  page 144)
1¾ ounces labneh or yogurt
1¾ ounces cherry tomatoes, chopped
1¾ ounces cucumber, chopped
a handful of mixed herbs, such as flat-
  leaf parsley and cilantro
1 small red onion, thinly sliced
⅔ cup drained canned or jarred
  chickpeas
a handful of baby spinach
a small handful of seeds and nuts—
  I use hemps seeds and toasted
  almonds

**VE** Opt for vegan yogurt.
**GF** Use a gluten-free grain such as buckwheat or brown rice.

Preheat the oven to 350°F. Line a baking sheet with parchment paper.

Put the mixed vegetables in a bowl, drizzle with olive oil and the harissa, and toss to coat. Arrange on the lined baking sheet in a single layer, season lightly with salt, and bake for 50 minutes, flipping the vegetables over halfway through. Remove from the oven and let cool. Drizzle with more olive oil and the lemon juice, then taste and adjust the seasoning with salt.

You will need a clean glass jar, about 1½ pints in capacity. Layer the ingredients in the jar, starting with the cooked grains. Top with the tahini sauce and labneh or yogurt, then the grilled vegetables, followed by the tomatoes, cucumber, herbs, onion, and chickpeas. Finish with the spinach and the seeds and nuts. Seal the jar and keep in the fridge until it's time to leave for your party. It will keep for a day in the fridge.

# Cauliflower Crust Pizza with Mozzarella, Spinach, and Egg

MAKES 1 PIZZA

CAULIFLOWER CRUST:

3½ ounces cauliflower, broken into
  florets
1½ ounces Parmesan or rawmesan (see
  page 28), finely grated
¾ cup plus 2 tablespoons almond or rice
  flour or other gluten-free flour
½ teaspoon dried oregano
½ teaspoon red pepper flakes
½ teaspoon salt
1 medium organic egg

TOPPINGS:

a handful of baby spinach leaves
5¼ ounces mozzarella, torn or sliced, or
  vegan soft cheese
1 medium organic egg

TO SERVE:

pickled or raw red onion
fresh basil leaves
salt and freshly ground black pepper,
  to taste
extra-virgin olive oil

Yes, you can also make a pizza crust with vegetables, and it's delicious! Here I've used cauliflower for a gluten-free alternative to the spelt and wheat pizza dough (see page 143), which I've topped with creamy mozzarella, spinach, and egg. I prefer to bake this in a kitchen oven because the temperature is more controlable for prebaking the pizza crust. But you can use an outdoor wood-fired stone pizza oven, as long as you keep a very close eye on the crust to avoid burning.

---

If using a wood-fired oven, light a fire 2 hours before baking. If using an indoor oven, preheat the oven to 480°F or its highest setting. Lay a sheet of parchment paper on a baking sheet.

Put the cauliflower in a food processor and process until it is finely ground but not mushy. Transfer to a mixing bowl, add all the remaining crust ingredients, and mix together into a dough.

Flatten and press the dough into a round on the lined baking sheet. Bake for 10 minutes if using an indoor oven. If using an outdoor stone pizza oven, bake for a maximum of 1 minute or until the crust has firmed. Remove from the oven, add the spinach, then the mozzarella, and finally the egg. Salt and pepper lightly. Bake for an additional 30 to 40 seconds until the egg is firm. If using an indoor oven, bake until the egg has firmed. Remove from the oven and sprinkle with pickled red onion, basil, and salt and pepper to taste, then drizzle with extra-virgin olive oil.

VE Opt for rawmesan (see page 28) and
vegan egg replacer for the pizza crust; opt for
vegan cheese for topping and omit the egg.
GF ✓

---

## Making homemade gluten-free flour

*Buying a bag of nut, seed, or oat flour is pricy compared to buying the ingredient whole and grinding it yourself at home. Simply use a coffee grinder or a powerful blender to grind your chosen nuts, seeds, or oats for 20 seconds or until they are finely ground, but be careful not to overgrind, or they will turn into a buttery paste!*

# Halloumi Veggie Skewers with Watermelon Buckwheat Salad

SERVES 4

WATERMELON AND BUCKWHEAT SALAD
2 cups water
⅔ cup buckwheat
3½ ounces baby spinach or arugula
1 red onion, sliced
7 ounces watermelon, diced
3½ ounces tomatillos or cherry
    tomatoes, halved
2 tablespoons minced fresh herbs, such
    as cilantro, parsley, or mint
2 tablespoons lemon juice
2 tablespoons extra-virgin olive oil
salt, to taste

HALLOUMI VEGGIE SKEWERS:
10½ ounces halloumi cheese or
    mushrooms, cut into bite-size pieces
8 small or 2 medium red or yellow
    peppers, cored, seeded and cut
    into bite-size pieces
4 small red onions, cut into
    bite-size pieces
2 green tomatillos (or substitute yellow
    tomatoes if you can't source)
7 ounces cauliflower florets
8 radishes
olive oil, for drizzling
salt and freshly ground black pepper,
    to taste

CREAMY RED PEPPER SAUCE:
½ red chile, chopped
2 roasted red peppers from a jar, drained
2 garlic cloves, chopped
1 cup walnuts
3 tablespoons water
2 tablespoons extra-virgin olive oil
juice of 1 lime
1 teaspoon honey or agave syrup
salt and freshly ground black pepper,
    to taste

**One of the easiest ways of cooking vegetables on the grill is to thread them onto skewers—ideal for preparing at home and transporting to a barbecue party. I love to combine a mix of vegetables with something powerfully savory in flavor such as halloumi cheese or mushrooms. Serve these skewers with creamy red pepper sauce and a refreshing watermelon and buckwheat salad. Naturally, you can vary the skewered vegetables based on season and availabilty.**

Heat a gas or charcoal grill. Bring the water to a boil and cook the buckwheat for 10 minutes. Drain. Transfer to a bowl and add the remaining watermelon and buckwheat salad ingredients; set aside until ready to serve. Put all the ingredients for the creamy red pepper sauce in a blender or food processor and blend until smooth. Transfer to a bowl and cover tightly or put in an airtight container and refrigerate until ready to serve.

For the skewers, put the halloumi or mushrooms with the prepared vegetables in a bowl, drizzle with olive oil, and sprinkle with salt and pepper to taste, then toss to coat. Thread the halloumi or mushrooms onto skewers, alternating with the vegetables.

When the coals of your charcoal grill have burnt down or your gas grill is hot, place the skewers on the grill grate and grill for a few minutes, turning frequently, until charred on all sides. Serve the skewers with the watermelon and buckwheat salad and creamy red pepper sauce.

VE Opt for mushrooms for the skewers, and
agave syrup for the creamy red pepper sauce.
GF ✓

# Eggplant Kebab with Rainbow Salad, Garlic Sauce, Hummus, and Flatbreads

SERVES 4
2 medium eggplants, cut into chunks

MARINADE:
2 tablespoons olive oil
1 teaspoon lemon juice
2 teaspoons ground cumin
1 teaspoon ground coriander
1 teaspoon red pepper flakes
1 teaspoon ground cinnamon
¾ teaspoon salt

GARLIC SAUCE:
6 tablespoons olive oil
5 garlic cloves, crushed
2 tablespoons plain yogurt
1 teaspoon agave syrup or honey
¾ teaspoon salt, or more to taste

RAINBOW SALAD
2 avocados, diced
1 small red onion, thinly sliced
3½ ounces red or white cabbage,
    shredded
3½ ounces cherry tomatoes, halved
1 red pepper, cut into strips
2¼ cups baby spinach
a handful of flat-leaf parsley and mint
    leaves, coarsely chopped
a handful of fresh herbs, such as cilantro,
    mint, and parsley
a handful of toasted almonds or
    other nuts

TO SERVE:
4 flatbreads
Classic Hummus (see page 34)
harissa
lemon wedges, for squeezing

Yottam Ottolenghi once told me that the best flavors are the bold and simple ones that you find in street food, such as from kebab stalls, and for that reason this is where many culinary stars go to eat. I don't need convincing because I already love pita bread stuffed with falafel and garlic sauce. As a variation on that theme, here we have eggplants grilled on skewers, marinated in spices such as cumin, ground coriander, and chile to give them a scrumptious flavor, and served with a refreshing minty cucumber salad. You can skip the bread and serve the dish in bowls, and also vary the veggies for grilling.

To prepare the kebabs, mix together all the ingredients for the marinade in a small bowl. Put the eggplants in a bowl, pour over the marinade, and toss to coat. Set aside to marinate at room temperature for 30 minutes, or cover and refrigerate for up to a day.

When getting ready to serve, using an immersion blender or a food processor, blend together all the ingredients for the garlic sauce until well combined. Set aside. Mix together the ingredients for the rainbow salad in a separate bowl.

Heat a charcoal or gas grill until hot. Alternatively, heat a grill pan on the stovetop over high heat. Thread the vegetables onto skewers and grill for 2 to 4 minutes on a charcoal or gas grill, or 3 to 5 minutes on a grill pan, or longer if needed in either case, turning frequently to cook evenly on all sides.

Serve the eggplant in flatbreads with the hummus and harissa, along with the garlic sauce and the rainbow salad.

VE Opt for vegan yogurt and agave syrup
for the sauce.
GF Use gluten-free flatbreads or omit.

# Green Crêpe Cake with Homemade Chocolate Spread and Chia Jam

―――――

MAKES 1 CAKE/SERVES 4 TO 6

GREEN CRÊPE MIXTURE
1½ cups spelt or all-purpose flour
pinch of salt
1⅔ cups plant-based or dairy milk
3 eggs or egg replacers like aquafaba
2 handfuls of fresh spinach
vegetable oil, for frying

HOMEMADE CHOCOLATE SPREAD
1½ cups raw hazelnuts
3½ ounces quality organic chocolate
    (70% cacao), in pieces

CHIA JAM
7 ounces raspberries or strawberries or
    other berries
1 tablespoon agave syrup
3 tablespoons water
2 tablespoons chia seeds

CHOCOLATE AND MASCARPONE CREAM
7 ounces homemade chocolate spread
12 ounces mascarpoone

TOPPING:
1 teaspoon raw cacao powder or
    cocoa powder

**Pancakes or crêpes are the perfect picnic or potluck food, easily prepared at home. They can be used both as savory-filled crêpes or as the base for a crêpe cake that you can quickly assemble wherever you are, with the addition of delicious layer fillings such as homemade Nutella mixed with a creamy mascarpone or cashew cream and chia jam that you bring with you in sealed containers—in a flash you have an impressive cake. You can easily prepare the pancakes and the fillings a day ahead. These crêpes are made with the addtion of spinach, turning them vibrantly green!**

―――

For the chocolate spread, preheat the oven to 400°F and roast the hazelnuts for 10 minutes. Let them cool and place the hazelnuts in a clean dish towel. Fold the towel over the hazelnuts and twist the end to make a little sack, and rub the hazelnuts from the outside of the towel with your hands, so that the skins easily come off the nuts. Open the towel and place the hazelnuts in a food processor (save a few for decoration), discarding the skins. Pulse for 5 minutes, stopping occasionally to scrape down the processor bowl.

In a small saucepan, melt the chocolate bar, let it cool slightly, and pour it into the food processor with the hazelnuts. Process until smooth and creamy.

For the chia jam, blend the ingredients together in a food processor. Transfer to a sterile jar and refrigerate overnight. The chia jam keeps for 1 week in the fridge.

For the chocolate and mascarpone cream, mix the ingredients together with a spoon in a small bowl. Transfer to a sealed container and store in the fridge.

For the crêpes, blend the ingredients, except the oil, into a smooth mixture. Heat a skillet and add a drizzle of vegetable oil. Pour in the crêpe batter to make a round pancake with a diameter of 5 to 6 inches. Fry until the crêpe has firmed, then flip it over and fry the other side. There should be enough mixture to make 6 crêpe. Transfer to a plate and repeat until the batter is finished. Store the crêpe, covered, in the fridge if you are not making the cake right away.

To make the cake, organize your workspace with one plate (or cake stand) in front of you, with the fillings and toppings within reach. Place a crêpe on the plate and spread with the chocolate and mascarpone cream. Add another crêpe and spread the chia jam on top, then add another crêpe and spread chocolate and mascarpone cream over that. Repeat until the last crêpe. Top with chocolate and mascarpone cream, dust with cacao powder, and decorate with the reserved roasted hazelnuts.

**Tip**
*Use pre-roasted hazelnuts to skip a step making the homemade chocolate spread.*

**VE** Use a vegan egg replacer.
**GF** Use a gluten-free flour.

# 8. PLATED

For an intimate dinner, carefully prepared and plated dishes can
feel more special and less distracting than a buffet of shared dishes.
Here is a selection of mains that balance texture and flavor
in each individual serving, where creamy meets crispy, smoky meets
fresh, and sweet meets savory. Let's get creative!

# Smoky Shiitake with Pea Farrotto and Chai Tea Sauce

SERVES 4

PEA FARROTTO:

¾ cup peas, fresh or frozen

2½ cups vegetable stock

olive oil or butter, for frying

3 garlic cloves, minced

2 cups semi-pearled farro

1¼ cups white wine

3 tablespoons olive oil

2½ ounces Parmesan, grated, or rawmesan (see page 28), plus extra to serve

salt and freshly ground black pepper, to taste

SMOKY SHIITAKE:

1 tablespoon ghee or olive oil

½ teaspoon liquid smoke (optional)

10½ ounces shiitake mushrooms (or use oyster or portobello mushrooms), sliced

1 teaspoon toasted sesame oil

salt and freshly ground black pepper, to taste

CHAI TEA SAUCE:

¾ cup chai tea

½ teaspoon honey or agave syrup

salt and freshly ground black pepper, to taste

Peas and mushrooms are both fantastic ingredients and they complement each other perfectly in this dish. Not just highly versatile in cooking, peas are also rich in plant-based protein. And while mushrooms have been valued for their medicinal properties throughout history, it's their powerful umami flavor that is the winning quality in a plant-based diet.

These mushrooms are fried with half a teaspoon of liquid smoke, an ingredient used in gastronomic cooking. Liquid smoke is available in speciality cooking stores and online. Teas are essentially aromatic herbs and flowers and, when used in cooking, they add a beautiful and subtle flavor. Here chai tea is used to complement the savory shiitake and farotto. You can also make the sauce with Earl Grey or Lapsang Souchong; the latter adds an extra-smoky flavor to the sauce.

To make the pea farotto, put the green peas in a blender with 6 tablespoons of the stock and mix to a coarse, crumbly texture, or mash together with a fork in a bowl. Set aside.

Heat a saucepan over medium-high heat. Add a drizzle of olive oil or a little butter and fry the garlic for a few seconds. Add the farro and fry, stirring, for 1 to 2 minutes. Stir in the wine and the rest of the vegetable stock and bring to a boil, then reduce the heat to low and simmer gently for 35 to 40 minutes, stirring frequently. Taste to see if the farro is tender, and if not, cook for a little longer.

Add the pea puree, olive oil, and Parmesan or Rawmesan and stir to combine, then season to taste with salt and pepper. Turn off the heat and cover the pan with a lid, then reheat just before serving.

Heat a skillet over medium-high heat. Add the ghee or olive oil and liquid smoke and fry the mushrooms for 2 minutes without stirring. Then fry, stirring, for an additional 2 to 3 minutes or until the excess moisture has evaporated. Drizzle with the toasted sesame oil and season to taste with salt and pepper.

Remove the mushrooms and quickly pour the chai tea into the pan, whisking to combine the remaining flavors of the mushrooms with the tea. Add the honey or agave syrup and whisk it into the sauce. Taste and adjust with salt and pepper.

Serve the pea farrotto topped with the mushrooms and a drizzle of the chai tea sauce. You can top with extra Parmesan or rawmesan, if you like.

VE Opt for olive oil for frying, and rawmesan instead of Parmesan.

GF Use brown rice or buckwheat instead of farro, adjusting the cooking times of the grains according to the package instructions.

# Caramelized Fennel Chops
# with Pumpkin Puree

SERVES 4

PUMPKIN PUREE:
1 small (about 10-ounce) pumpkin or
   butternut squash, halved, seeds and
   membrane removed
2½ tablespoons olive oil
salt and freshly ground black pepper

4 small fennel bulbs, fronds and the
   rougher outer layer cut off
2 garlic cloves, minced
2 tablespoons olive oil
1 tablespoon balsamic vinegar
1 teaspoon ground fennel seeds
1 teaspoon thyme leaves
olive oil, for frying
1½ tablespoons coconut sugar
⅓ teaspoon salt
fresh thyme sprigs, to serve

RED WINE SAUCE
6 tablespoons red wine
1 tablespoon olive oil
salt and freshly ground black pepper,
   to taste

**Caramelizing vegetables adds extra gloss and char to the juicy flavors. This plate combines the sweetness of pumkin puree with garlic and balsamic glazed fennel chops. Keep the stem of the fennel during the cooking to hold the fennel together in a "chop," though discard it when you eat. I love the simple way of making this quick sauce, adding liquid to the pan to absorb the residues of caramelization—no flavor is wasted.**

Preheat the oven to 325°F. Place the pumpkin in a baking dish. Roast for 50 minutes to 1 hour. Remove from the oven (but keep the oven on) and scrape the flesh out. Transfer to a food processor. Blend with the olive oil and taste and adjust with salt and pepper.

Quarter the fennels lengthwise, including the stems. Mix the garlic, olive oil, balsamic vinegar, fennel seeds, and thyme in a small bowl.

Heat a big skillet and add a generous drizzle of olive oil. Add the coconut sugar and salt and stir for a minute, lower the heat and place the pieces of fennel, cut-side down without overlapping, in the pan (fry in two batches). Cook the fennel until it's transparent and golden, 2 to 3 minutes on each side. When the fennel is cooked and golden, remove from the pan (but don't wash the pan), place in a bowl, and drizzle with the garlic mixture.

Line a baking sheet with parchment paper and roast the fennel in the oven for 8 to 10 minutes.

Meanwhile, reheat the pan that you used to caramelize the fennel. Pour in the red wine and olive oil. Whisk the liquid and combine with the caramelized residue in the pan, infusing the sauce with flavor. Season to taste.

When the fennel is roasted, quickly reheat the pumkin puree in a small saucepan and serve with the fennel on a plate. Drizzle over a spoonful of the red wine sauce and top with thyme sprigs.

VE ✓
GF ✓

# Hot and Smoky Seitan Sausages with Red Cabbage Cider Confit and Green Mash

SERVES 4

**SEITAN SAUSAGES:**

ghee or olive oil, for frying

3½ ounces shiitake mushrooms, sliced

2 garlic cloves, minced

1½ cups drained canned beans, such as
  cannellini or other white beans

1 tablespoon smoked paprika

3 tablespoons nutritional yeast or finely
  grated Parmesan

2 tablespoons shoyu soy sauce or tamari

14 ounces seitan, drained

1 teaspoon liquid smoke

1 tablespoon chipotle paste or other chile
  paste, or more to taste

5 tablespoons rice flour

1 tablespoon olive oil

1 teaspoon dried oregano

½ teaspoon salt, or more to taste

**RED CABBAGE CIDER CONFIT:**

olive oil or ghee, for frying

1 red onion, thinly sliced

14 ounces red cabbage, finely shredded

½ apple, cored and thinly sliced

1 teaspoon salt, or more to taste

1¼ cups apple cider

1¼ cups water

2 tablespoons red wine vinegar

**FOR THE GREEN MASH:**

4 cups broccoli florets

1 tablespoon tahini

2½ tablespoons olive oil

1 garlic clove, minced

1 teaspoon lemon juice

salt and freshly ground black pepper,
  to taste

**MUSTARD MAYONNAISE:**

3½ ounces mayonnaise

2½ tablespoons Dijon mustard

pickled red onion, to serve (optional)

**Serving a fancy sausage and mash plate is both fun and delicious. The sausages are made with seitan, which has the perfect texture and binding quality, spiced with smoked paprika, chipotle paste, and liquid smoke for a robust flavor. They are served with broccoli mash along with a colorful cabbage confit and a mustard-enhanced mayo.**

For the sausages, heat a skillet over medium-high heat. Add a little ghee or a drizzle of olive oil and fry the shiitake with the garlic for 7 to 8 minutes until they have shrunk in size and the excess liquid has reduced, stirring to avoid burning.

Transfer with all the remaining sausage ingredients to a food processor and process until smooth. Taste and adjust the seasoning with salt and chipotle paste if needed. Shape into 8 to 10 sausages. Wrap each sausage in foil or plastic wrap and chill in the fridge for 1 hour or up to 24 hours.

Meanwhile, make the red cabbage cider confit. Heat a skillet with a lid over medium-high heat. Add a generous drizzle of oil or equivalent quantity of ghee and fry the onion, stirring, for 3 to 4 minutes. Add the cabbage and fry, stirring, for 5 minutes. Stir in all the remaining confit ingredients and cover the pan with the lid. Reduce the heat and simmer gently for 35 to 40 minutes, stirring occasionally.

Meanwhile, make the green mash. Steam the broccoli florets for 4 minutes. Transfer to a food processor and blend until smooth with the rest of the ingredients. Taste and adjust with salt and pepper.

Preheat the oven to 350°F. Unwrap the sausages, place on a baking sheet and bake for 30 minutes until golden brown, turning occasionally. Alternatively, heat a skillet over medium-high heat and fry the sausages for a few minutes, turning frequently, until golden brown.

While the sausages are cooking, mix the mayonnaise and mustard together in a small bowl. Quickly reheat the green mash. Serve the sausages with the green mash, red cabbage cider confit, mustard mayonnaise, and pickled red onion, if you like.

**VE** Opt for nutritional yeast, olive oil
for frying, and vegan mayonnaise.
**GF** This recipe is not gluten-free.

### Tip

*You can also make super-delicious croquettes with the same mixture by rolling the sausages in panko breadcrumbs and frying in the same way as for the Croquettes on page 165. Another way to serve the sausages is in hot dog buns, substituting coleslaw for the confit, or try serving the sausages with chutney and top-quality ketchup. You can also buy plant-based sausage skins to stuff, in stores specializing in vegan food or online.*

# Croquettes with Mustard Mayo

SERVES 4

CROQUETTES:

1¾ pounds medium to small waxy
  potatoes
3 organic egg yolks
6 tablespoons dairy or plant-based milk
2½ ounces Parmesan, finely grated, or
  rawmesan (see page 28)
1 teaspoon salt
¼ teaspoon ground white pepper
3 medium organic eggs
¾ cup flour of choice
1¼ cups panko breadcrumbs
vegetable oil, for frying

MUSTARD MAYONNAISE:

7 ounces mayonnaise
1 tablespoon Dijon mustard

TO SERVE:

4 small slices of sourdough, toasted
pickled red onion
avocado slices
fresh herbs, such as chives, dill, or
  parsley (optional)

**Croquettes are a star when it comes to texture, with their crusty exterior and soft, creamy inside. But forget the artificial taste of processed fast-food croquettes—this upmarket version is in another league.**

**Mustard mayo is the ideal accompaniment for the crispy balls, along with rustic sourdough toast, but you can easily serve the croquettes with just a simple green salad. The croquettes are also delicious with a garlic sauce or garlic butter with fresh herbs.**

___

For the croquettes, preheat the oven to 350°F. Line a baking sheet with parchment paper. Place the potatoes on the lined baking sheet and bake for 50 minutes. Remove from the oven and let cool, then cut in half and scoop out the flesh, discarding the skins. Mash in a bowl. Whisk together the egg yolks and milk, then stir into the mash with the Parmesan or rawmesan, salt, and white pepper. Form the mixture into oval-shaped balls, place on a baking sheet, and chill in the fridge for 1 to 2 hours.

Preheat the oven to 225°F. Line a baking sheet with parchment paper. Mix the mayonnaise and mustard together in a small bowl.

Beat together the eggs in one bowl, put the flour in a second bowl, and put the breadcrumbs in another. Add a generous drizzle of oil to a skillet and heat over medium-high heat. First roll the balls in flour, then dip in the beaten egg, then roll in the breadcrumbs to coat. Fry, in batches, for 3 to 4 minutes, turning regularly for even cooking. Remove from the oil and drain on paper towels to absorb the excess oil. Transfer the fried croquettes to the lined baking sheet and keep warm in the oven while you finish frying the remaining croquettes.

Serve the warm croquettes with the mustard mayonnaise, along with the sourdough toast, pickled red onion, avocado, and a few herbs.

___

**VE** Use vegan mayonnaise, rawmesan instead of Parmesan for
the croquettes, and plant-based milk, and omit the egg yolks
and eggs altogether. Skip rolling the croquettes in flour and
egg, and go straight to coating with panko before frying.
**GF** Use gluten-free flour and breadcrumbs, and toasted rustic
gluten-free bread.

# Miso-Glazed Eggplant with Furikake Rice

SERVES 4

1 cup Japanese or sushi rice

2 small eggplants

sesame or vegetable oil, for frying

sesame seeds, black or white or a mix,
  for sprinkling

FURIKAKE (MAKES ABOUT 1½ CUPS):

1 toasted nori sheet, ½ minced,
  ½ cut into thin, short strips and
  reserved for garnish

½ cup white sesame seeds, toasted

½ cup black sesame seeds

1 teaspoon shichimi togarashi or red
  pepper flakes

2 tablespoons shoyu soy sauce or tamari

2 tablespoons coconut sugar

MISO GLAZE:

3½ ounces red miso paste or use another
  miso of your choice

2 tablespoons mirin

1 tablespoon agave syrup or maple syrup

TO SERVE (OPTIONAL):

Japanese Pickles (see page 128)

Wakame Salad (see page 128)

Carrot ribbons

**This popular Japanese dish, known as nasu dengaku, dates back hundreds of years and demonstrates how eggplant magically transforms from drab to delicious under the broiler. The miso glaze adds a savory hit without using salt itself, and is contrasted by sweetness from the agave or maple syrup for an extra-tasty result. When mixing the glaze, taste and adjust the balance of savory and sweet, adding more syrup, if needed.**

To make the furikake, put the minced nori in a food processor with all the remaining furikake ingredients and process until well combined. Transfer to a sterilized jar, seal, and keep in the fridge for up a week.

Rinse and cook the rice according to the instructions on page 16 (onigiri).

Meanwhile, cut the eggplants in half lengthwise and make crosshatched cuts in the flesh of each half. Put all the ingredients for the miso glaze in a bowl and whisk until combined.

Preheat the broiler or preheat the oven to 465°F. Line a baking sheet with parchment paper. Heat a skillet that has a lid over medium-high heat. Add a drizzle of oil and fry the rounded side of the eggplant halves for 3 to 4 minutes until the skin is shriveled. Flip the eggplant halves over, cut-side down, cover the pan with the lid, and fry for 3 minutes. Transfer the eggplant halves, cut-side up, to the lined baking sheet and brush generously with the miso glaze. Broil for 3 to 4 minutes or until the glaze has caramelized.

Sprinkle the cooked rice with sesame seeds and 2 tablespoons of the furikake (and put extra furikake on the table) and garnish with the reserved nori strips and carrot ribbons. Serve with the eggplant, along with the pickles and wakame salad, if you like.

**VE** Make your own furikake or look for fish-free furikake if buying ready-made.

**GF** Opt for gluten-free tamari.

## Using miso

*Miso paste is made by fermenting soy beans, or sometimes rice or other grains, resulting in an intensely savory, naturally salty flavor. Miso can be added to either liquids or fat and used in marinades and sauces or soups and stews as you would soy sauce. Varieties of miso range from light to dark; the darker the miso, the stronger the flavor, with white miso being mild enough to be used in desserts.*

# Faux Fishcakes with Almond Sesame Dip

SERVES 4

ALMOND SESAME DIP:
2 tablespoons almond butter
1½ tablespoons toasted sesame oil
1½ tablespoons shoyu soy or
    tamari sauce
2 tablespoons fresh lime juice
1 teaspoon honey or agave syrup

FAUX FISHCAKES:
9 ounces smoked tofu
2½ tablespoons shoyu soy or
    tamari sauce
a handful of cilantro
1½ tablespoons minced seaweed—I use
    nori or hijiki, but any kind will do
1 teaspoon honey or agave syrup
2 scallions, chopped
2 garlic cloves, crushed
1 tablespoon sriracha sauce
2 teaspoons finely grated fresh ginger
1 cup cooked brown rice
salt, to taste
sesame or vegetable oil, for frying

TO SERVE:
10½ ounces mixed vegetables and
    fruit, such as carrot, cucumber, and
    radishes, peeled and/or seeded as
    appropriate and cut into bite-size
    pieces
drizzles of sweet rice vinegar
    (sushi vinegar)
sesame seeds, for sprinkling

**This recipe makes a great dinner dish and has been a favorite in our house for many years. The combination of seaweed and smoked tofu gives the cakes a seafood-like flavor, with cilantro, ginger, and soy adding an Asian-style freshness and fragrance. The cakes are made even more scrumptious by being dunked in an almond sesame dip.**

Combine all the ingredients for the almond sesame dip in a pitcher and blend with an immersion blender until well combined.

Put all the ingredients for the faux fishcakes, except the oil, in a food processor and process until well combined. Taste and adjust the seasoning with salt. Shape the mixture into 12 small cakes, place on a baking sheet, and chill in the fridge for 30 minutes. Preheat the oven to 225°F. Line a baking sheet with parchment paper.

Heat a skillet over medium heat. Add a drizzle of oil and fry the cakes in batches, a couple at a time with ample space between the cakes, for 2 to 3 minutes on each side until golden brown. Transfer the fried cakes to the lined baking sheet and keep warm in the oven while you finish frying the remainder.

Divide the cakes among four plates and arrange the cut vegetables decoratively and drizzle with a little sweet rice vinegar. Drizzle with the almond sesame dip and sprinkle with sesame seeds.

**VE** Opt for agave syrup.
**GF** Opt for gluten-free tamari.

# Baked Polenta with Caponata and Roasted Beets

SERVES 4

ROASTED BEETS:

4 small beets, scrubbed and
    quartered
1 tablespoon balsamic vinegar
1 tablespoon olive oil
salt and freshly ground black pepper

POLENTA:

4 cups water
1½ cups polenta (not the quick-cook
    type)
3 tablespoons olive oil
2½ ounces Parmesan, grated, or
    rawmesan (see page 28)
salt and freshly ground black pepper, to
    taste

CAPONATA:

olive oil, for frying
1 eggplant, diced
2 celery stalks, finely chopped
2 red peppers, cored, seeded and cut into
    small pieces
2 best-quality tomatoes, chopped
2 garlic cloves, crushed
1 red onion, finely chopped
1¾ ounces black olives, halved and
    pitted
a handful of flat-leaf parsley,
    minced
2 teaspoons dried oregano
½ cup plus 2 tablespoons water
¾ cup tomato sauce
3 tablespoons red wine vinegar
2 or 3 Medjool dates, pitted and minced
    (or a handful of dried fruit, finely
    chopped)
2 teaspoons salt
¼ teaspoon freshly ground
    black pepper

This meal is the perfect Sunday lunch or dinner, especially served
with a good red wine or a fine hard cider. Polenta, originating from Italy,
is made from cornmeal and is traditionally cooked with lengthy stirring
on the stovetop. It's becoming increasingly popular to bake polenta in
the oven, which means less stirring but the baking process also adds
extra deliciousness. The polenta is baked until firm. I use cookie
cutters to cut out a round portion for each plate; you can also cut the
polenta into squares. If you would like a creamy polenta, bake only for
30 minutes. I've topped it here with another Italian classic—caponata—
and roasted beets.

Preheat the oven to 350°F. Line a shallow baking pan with parchment paper.
In a bowl, toss the beet with olive oil, balsamic vinegar, and salt and pepper.
Set aside.

To make the polenta, bring the water to a boil in a large saucepan. Slowly
pour in the polenta while whisking vigorously to avoid lumps forming. When
the mixture is smooth, reduce the heat and simmer for 5 minutes, whisking
constantly. Stir in the olive oil and Parmesan or rawmesan, then taste and
adjust the seasoning with salt and pepper. Pour the polenta into the lined
baking dish and bake for 40 minutes for firm polenta. For creamy polenta,
bake for 25 to 30 minutes.

Place the beets on a separate baking sheet in the oven at the same time
and bake for 40 minutes, check their doneness and extend the baking
time a few minutes, if needed.

Meanwhile, make the caponata. Heat a skillet over medium-high heat.
Add a generous drizzle of olive oil and fry the vegetables, olives, and herbs
together for 15 to 20 minutes, stirring frequently, until fragrant and golden.
Stir in the water, tomato sauce, vinegar, and dates and season with salt and
pepper. Reduce the heat to low and let the caponata simmer gently for 20
minutes, stirring occasionally to avoid sticking on the bottom of the pan.

Remove the polenta from the oven. If you opted for firm polenta, cut it
into portions using a knife or cookie cutter. If you opted for creamy polenta,
use a big spoon to scoop the polenta onto the plates. Top with the caponata
and roasted beets.

VE Opt for rawmesan.
GF ✓

# 9. SWEET ENDINGS

This chapter could just as easily have been titled "Sweet Beginnings," as in my home country
of Sweden it is a traditional part of everyday life that we get together and share a sweet treat,
a custom we call fika. So for my fellow Swedes in particular, I have included a recipe for babka,
which is similar in flavor to our traditional Swedish cinnamon rolls but a bit heavier on the spice!
For the ideal dessert for warmer days, chill out in style with my exotic freezer mango cheesecake
or some intriguing-tasting and -looking homemade ice cream with black sesame seeds.
But if you're wanting something cozy and comforting instead, indulge in the chai-flavored carrot
cake or waffles with berries and caramel sauce.
For a light and delicate dessert, my panna cotta made with coconut cream
and green matcha tea powder will fit the bill perfectly.

# Matcha Coconut Panna Cotta

SERVES 4

**PANNA COTTA:**
½ teaspoon agar agar powder
2 tablespoons water
2 teaspoons green matcha tea powder,
   plus extra for sprinkling (optional—
   or choose from the other flavoring
   options)
1⅔ cups full-fat coconut milk
2 tablespoons honey or agave syrup
¼ teaspoon vanilla extract, or 1 vanilla
   bean, split lengthwise and seeds
   scraped out

**FLAVORING OPTIONS:**
2 tablespoons pureed mango
1 teaspoon freshly brewed strong coffee
1 teaspoon finely grated lime zest
1 teaspoon rum
2 tablespoons pureed raspberries
1 teaspoon rose water or rose syrup or
   other flower extract

**TO SERVE:**
agave syrup
sprinkle of bee pollen (optional)
black sesame seeds or toasted
   crushed nuts

**This dessert literally melts in your mouth, as its texture is so refined and silky. While traditional panna cotta is made with dairy and gelatin, this version combines coconut milk and agar agar to create a fully plant-based alternative. I've added green matcha tea powder for an interesting twist, but you can skip it to create a classic white panna cotta if you prefer. It's easy to make variations of this dessert by simply substituting another flavor for the matcha—see the ingredient list for suggestions. You can of course use heavy cream instead of coconut milk.**

———

Mix the agar agar powder with the water and matcha powder in a small bowl until well blended. Place a small saucepan over low heat. Add the agar agar mixture and all the remaining panna cotta ingredients, including your choice of flavoring, and simmer gently for 1 to 2 minutes. Pour the warm mixture into four molds (I use individual muffin cups, but ramekins or other round small molds will also work) and allow to cool. Chill in the fridge for 1½ hours. Remove from the fridge and invert each mold in turn onto a serving plate, then lift away the mold to reveal the panna cotta.

   Serve with a drizzle of agave syrup and a pinch of crunchy toppings like sprinkles of bee pollen, black sesame seeds, or toasted crushed nuts.

**VE** Opt for agave syrup.
**GF** ✓

---

**Tip**
*Matcha powder varies greatly in quality and price. The finest matcha is handpicked and designated as 'ceremonial grade', the type used in traditional Japanese tea ceremonies, whereas cheaper and lower-quality matcha can be more bitter and 'off' in taste. So look for the ceremonial grade variety when buying matcha.*

# Sweet Tahini Babka

SERVES 6

½ cup warm (not hot) plant-based or
    dairy milk
2 teaspoons fast-action dried yeast
¼ cup coconut sugar
¼ teaspoon salt
2 cups spelt or all-purpose flour, plus
    extra for dusting
1 large organic egg
1 teaspoon vanilla extract
5 tablespoons butter, softened, or olive oil

ORANGE TAHINI CHOCOLATE SPREAD:

⅔ cup coconut sugar
3 tablespoons tahini
¼ cup raw cacao or cocoa powder
2 teaspoons ground cinnamon
4½ tablespoons butter, softened, or 5
    tablespoons olive oil, plus extra for
    greasing
pinch of salt
1 tablespoon grated orange zest

SWEET GLAZE:

1 tablespoon honey or agave syrup
2 tablespoons water

**Babka is Polish for "grandmother" and also the name of a classic Jewish sweet yeast bread. My first encounter with babka was in a Jewish café in Amsterdam, and it was instant love because it was so delicious and reminiscent of the cinnamon rolls of my childhood in Sweden. Popular fillings for babka are chocolate and cinnamon, but for this version I've added tahini for a sesame twist, which gives the sweet spread a slightly savory, nutty edge. Traditional babka recipes call for butter, making for a lovely rich taste, but you can use olive oil instead with excellent results and egg replacer for a vegan babka.**

––––

Whisk together the warm milk, yeast, and a pinch of the coconut sugar in a small bowl. Let stand for about 10 minutes to activate the yeast—you'll see it becoming foamy on the surface.

Mix together the remaining coconut sugar, the salt, and the flour in a large bowl, or in the bowl of a stand mixer fitted with the paddle attachment. In a separate bowl, beat together the egg and vanilla. Add the egg mixture to the flour while mixing constantly with your hands or with the mixer on low speed until incorporated. Add the yeast mixture and keep kneading while you gradually add the butter or olive oil, switching to the dough hook if using a mixer. Continue kneading on a floured work surface, if kneading by hand, until the dough is smooth. Grease a bowl with butter or olive oil, add the dough, and cover with a clean dish towel. Set aside to rise in a warm spot for 2 hours.

Meanwhile, line an 8½ by 4½-inch loaf pan with parchment paper. Mix together all the ingredients for the orange tahini chocolate spread in a bowl and set aside.

Roll the dough out on a work surface lightly dusted with flour into a large rectangle, ⅛ to ¼ inch thick. Spread with an even layer of the orange tahini chocolate spread. Starting from one longer side, roll up the dough into a long roll. Slice the roll in half lengthwise. Keeping the cut sides facing upward, wind the two long pieces of dough around each other to form a twisted rope, then place in the greased loaf pan. Tuck in the ends of the dough to neaten. Cover with a dish towel and set the babka aside to rise in a warm spot for 30 minutes to 1 hour.

Meanwhile, preheat the oven to 350°F. Put the honey or agave syrup and water for the glaze in a small saucepan and bring to a boil, stirring. Reduce the heat and simmer for a couple of minutes, then set aside.

Bake the babka for 30 minutes or until golden brown. Remove from the oven and brush with the glaze. Let cool in the pan before slicing and serving.

––––

**VE** Opt for plant-based milk, olive oil, vegan egg
replacer, and agave syrup.
**GF** The babka is not gluten-free.

# Black Sesame Ice Cream with Lime and Sea Salt

MAKES ABOUT 1 QUART

2 (14-ounce) cans full-fat coconut milk
2 tablespoons lime juice
¾ cup coconut sugar
¾ cup black sesame seeds
¾ cup raw cashew nuts, soaked in water
    for 2 to 4 hours and drained
1½ teaspoons vanilla extract
½ teaspoon sea salt
1 tablespoon arrowroot powder

CHOCOLATE DRIZZLE:

1¾ ounces good-quality organic dark
    chocolate, broken into pieces, or
    2 tablespoons unsweetened cocoa
    powder
2 tablespoons coconut oil
1 teaspoon agave syrup

TO SERVE:

cones (optional)
a handful of toasted nuts, crushed

Big in Japan but still a relatively rare sight in ice cream parlors in the West, this black sesame ice cream is certainly something else! Think ice-cold creamy and sweet tahini, and you're not far from imagining the taste. You can add a touch of edible charcoal powder to the ingredients for a true black color, but personally I love the minimal natural gray-beige look of this ice cream with the tiny speckles of black sesame seeds.

Put all the ingredients for the ice cream in a blender or food processor and blend until smooth—there will be tiny dots of black sesame seed visible in the mixture.

Transfer the ice cream mixture to a bowl, cover, and chill in the fridge for 30 minutes. Churn the mixture in an ice cream maker for 25 minutes or until firm and frozen. Transfer the ice cream to a freezer-safe container and freeze for 30 minutes before serving. It will keep in the freezer for up to 2 months.

Meanwhile, put the ingredients for the chocolate drizzle in a small saucepan and heat gently, stirring, until melted and well blended.

To serve, scoop the ice cream into cones or small bowls, drizzle with or dip into the chocolate drizzle, and sprinkle with or dip into the crushed nuts.

VE Use vegan chocolate.
GF Omit the cones and serve in bowls or cups.

# Ginger and Hibiscus Poached Pears with Ice Cream

SERVES 4

4 firm pears, peeled but stems left intact

4 cups strong-brewed hibiscus tea (let it
   steep for at least 10 minutes)

1 tablespoon pureed fresh ginger

1 teaspoon pureed lemongrass (optional)

2 tablespoons agave syrup

1 teaspoon vanilla extract

TO SERVE:

ice cream, mascarpone, or Whipped
   Coconut Cream (see page 185)

sprinkles of black sesame seeds

**Poached pears look and taste stunning and yet are simple to prepare. Here they are infused with hibiscus tea, aromatic fresh ginger, and hibiscus tea during the process. Serve with vanilla ice cream, mascarpone, or whipped coconut cream.**

Put the pears in a saucepan. Fill the saucepan with the hibiscus tea and add the pureed ginger, pureed lemongrass (if using), agave syrup, and vanilla. Bring to a boil, then reduce the heat and simmer for 30 minutes. Turn off the heat but keep the pears in the syrup until ready to serve. The pears can be poached up to 2 days in advance, then cooled and kept, tightly covered, in the fridge. Reheat gently before serving.

Carefully remove the pears from the syrup and serve with ice cream, mascarpone, or whipped coconut cream. Sprinkle with black sesame seeds.

**VE** Use vegan ice cream.

**GF** ✓

# -Bake Mango Cheesecake

SERVES 6

CRUST:

2 cups mixed toasted or raw nuts, such as
    almonds and cashew nuts, unsalted

1¼ cups Medjool dates, pitted and
    coarsely chopped

½ teaspoon sea salt

TOPPING:

3½ ounces mango pulp

2 tablespoons agave syrup

2 cups raw cashew nuts, soaked in water
    for 2 to 4 hours, then drained

1 teaspoon lime juice

3½ ounces coconut oil

**Semi-frozen no-bake cakes are my go-to choice for hot summer days, and this recipe is both vegan and gluten-free for maximum flexibility. The natural sweet stickiness of dates binds the nuts together for the crust, and adding a little salt gives it a slight caramel quality. The smooth, juicy mango filling makes a delicious contrast to the nutty base. Coconut oil is often used in raw cakes because it readily solidifies at low temperatures, so chilling the cake firms the filling nicely.**

To make the crust, put the nuts in a food processor and pulse until coarsely ground. Add the dates and salt and process until the mixture is sticky and grainy. Press into an even layer over the bottom of a 6- or 8-inch springform pan.

To make the topping, put all the topping ingredients except the coconut oil in a food processor and pulse briefly to combine. Add the coconut oil, in small quantities at a time, to the food processor and process until well blended. Pour over the crust and smooth the surface with a spatula. Freeze the cheesecake for at least 1 hour or until firm.

To serve, release the cheesecake from the pan and let stand at room temperature for 20 minutes.

VE ✓
GF ✓

# Sweet Mess with Salted Caramel

When you are catering for a number of people, serving an easy dessert gives you more time to enjoy being social. Here simple waffles are topped with fruit and berries and creamy ricotta, and drizzled with caramel sauce. You can serve whipped coconut cream or ice cream instead of ricotta.

SERVES 6

6 Waffles (see right), freshly made
7 ounces fresh berries or pieces of freshly cut fruit
300g ricotta or Whipped Coconut Cream (at right; optional)

SALTED CARAMEL SAUCE
1⅔ cups coconut milk or other mik
¾ cup coconut sugar or brown sugar
2 tablespoons raw cacao powder
1 teaspoon vanilla extract
⅓ teaspoon salt, plus more to taste
1 teaspoon mild olive oil or coconut oil

To make the salted caramel sauce, whisk the ingredients together in a heavy-bottomed pan and bring to a boil, then reduce the heat and simmer, stirring, for 5 minutes. Set aside. Place the waffles on a serving plate and top with fruit and berries. Drizzle with the caramel sauce and serve with ricotta, if desired.

**VE** Use coconut milk.
**GF** Make the waffles with gluten-free flour.

# Whipped Coconut Cream

Whipped dairy cream is easily swapped out for whipped coconut cream. Use thick full-fat coconut milk, not light or thinner coconut milk.

SERVES 4

1 cup full-fat coconut milk, refrigerated
1 tablespoon honey or agave syrup
1 teaspoon vanilla extract
½ teaspoon lemon juice

Whisk all the ingredients together. Place in the fridge until ready to serve.

**VE** ✓
**GF** ✓

# Waffles

Crispy waffles are the perfect companion to creamy mascarpone or whipped coconut cream and berries. These waffles are egg-free and suitable for vegans.

SERVES 4

3 tablespoons mild olive oil, plus extra for brushing
1¼ cups plant-based or dairy milk
1½ cups spelt or all-purpose flour or gluten-free flour
1 teaspoon baking powder
¼ teaspoon of salt
1 teaspoon vanilla extract
3 tablespoons coconut or brown sugar

Preheat the oven to 225°F. Line a baking sheet with parchment paper. Preheat a waffle maker. Mix all the ingredients together in a food processor. Brush the waffle maker with olive oil, then cook the waffles in batches, following the manufacturer's instructions, until golden brown and crisp. As you finish them, transfer the finished waffles to the lined baking sheet and keep warm in the oven while you cook the remaining batter.

**VE** ✓
**GF** Make the waffles using gluten-free flour.

# Chai Carrot Cake with Lime and Rose Frosting

Serves 6

CHAI CARROT CAKE:
coconut oil or butter, for greasing
1⅓ cups spelt flour
¾ teaspoon baking powder
¾ teaspoon baking soda
¾ teaspooon salt
1 teaspoon ground cinnamon
½ teaspoon ground cardamom
½ teaspoon ground ginger
¼ teaspoon ground nutmeg
pinch of freshly ground black pepper
¾ cup coconut sugar
½ cup olive oil
3 tablespoons agave syrup
1 teaspoon vanilla extract
2 medium organic eggs
¼ pound carrots, finely grated

LIME AND ROSE FROSTING:
5¼ ounces cream cheese or vegan crème
  fraîche or white cashew cream
1 teaspoon vanilla extract
1 teaspoon fresh lime juice
1½ tablespoons agave syrup
1½ teaspoons rose water (optional)

TO DECORATE
pomegranate seeds
rose petals, fresh or dried
hazlenuts or pistachio nuts

I have always had a soft spot for carrot cakes and this comforting spiced version is a regular on the table at home. Indian chai flavors of cinnamon, cardamom, and nutmeg work beautifully in baking, and here they bring a warmth to the juicy carrots. The sharp, floral-tasting frosting provides a delicious cool contrast to the spicy cake. You can extend the Indian theme by serving the cake with Mango Lassis (see page 33) or Golden Milk Lattes (see page 33).

Preheat the oven to 350°F. Grease an 8-inch round cake pan with coconut oil or butter, line the bottom and sides with parchment paper, and grease the parchment.

Put all the ingredients for the lime and rose frosting in a bowl and whisk together until light and creamy. Cover the bowl and refrigerate until ready to assemble the cake.

For the cake, sift the flour, baking powder, baking soda, salt, and spices into a large bowl and mix well. In another bowl, whisk together the coconut sugar, olive oil, agave syrup, and vanilla. While whisking constantly, add the eggs one by one (or, if using egg replacer, add half at a time). Pour the sugar-egg mixture into the flour mixture and mix together, then fold in the grated carrots.

Pour the cake batter into the prepared pan, level the top, and bake for 45 minutes or until a thin skewer inserted into the center of the cake comes out clean. Remove from the oven and let cool for 30 minutes in the pan. Turn the cake out of the pan and place on a serving plate. Spread the frosting over the top of the cake and sprinkle with pomegranate seeds, rose petals, and nuts.

VE Opt for vegan egg replacer for the cake, and vegan natural cream cheese and vegan crème fraîche for the frosting.
GF The cake is not gluten-free.

# INDEX

ajvar dip 138

almond butter: almond
    sesame dip 168
    lemon almond dressing 75

apple juice, warm mulled 55

artichoke dip, rainbow crudités with 34

asparagus: green garden salad 44

avocados: green garden salad 44
    Indian carrot salad 101
    jackfruit bulgogi salad 89
    mini Caesar salad baskets 28
    mint avocado smoothie 76
    new moon salad 76
    pumpkin, wild rice and lemongrass salad 87
    rainbow salad 153
    smörgåstårta 47
    tahini, sweet potato and avocado pizza 144
    wabi-sabi salad 80

babka, sweet tahini 176

bake-your-own pizza party 143

bananas: cauliflower smoothie 76
    midsummer dream cake 50

beans: hot and smoky seitan bangers 163
    new moon salad 76
    see also butter beans; cannellini beans

beets: baked polenta with caponata and
      roasted beets 171
    beet carrot smoothie 76
    beet ravioli 67

the big roast! 135
    date and beet chocolate cake 70
    goat's cheese and beet pizza 144
    herbed beet, lentil and feta salad 90 water-
    melon and Chioggia beet 83

berries: sweet mess 185

bibimbap bowls 109

the big roast! 135

black sesame ice cream 179

blackberry onion confit 55

bread: curried flatbread pizza 30
    Nordic nacho salad 86
    smörgåstårta 47
    sweet tahini babka 176

broccoli: broccoli and pesto pizza 146
    broccoli soup and feta cream 24
    crispy sesame broccoli 120
    green mash 163
    green pea and broccoli fritters 41

Brussels sprouts with pomegranate 64

buckwheat: watermelon buckwheat salad 150

bulgogi, jackfruit 125

butter beans: green garden salad 44

butternut squash: the big roast! 135

butternut squash boats 21
    lemongrass and butternut squash soup 139

cabbage: kimchi 109
    rainbow salad 153
    winter coleslaw 61
    see also cavolo nero; red cabbage

Caesar dressing 28

cakes: chai carrot cake 186
    date and beet chocolate cake 70
    green crêpe cake 154
    midsummer dream cake 50

cannellini beans: ribollita 103

caponata 171

caramel, salted 185

caramelised fennel chops 160

caramelised onion tarte tatin 22

carrots: beet carrot smoothie 76
    the big roast! 135
    chai carrot cake 186
    herbed beet, lentil and feta salad 90
    Indian carrot salad 101
    labneh and harissa-roasted carrots 132
    summer rolls 18

cashew nuts: black sesame ice cream 179
    cashew tahini sauce 61
    chocolate cashew butter cream 70
    coriander pesto 139
    lemony cashew cream 15
    no-bake mango cheesecake 182

cauliflower: cauliflower crust pizza 149
    cauliflower roast 61
    cauliflower smoothie 76
    halloumi veggie skewers 150
    tandoori cauliflower 101

cavolo nero: butternut squash boats 21
    garlic mushrooms and cavolo nero 104
    ribollita 103
    zucchini involtini 27

celeriac: hasselback celeriac roast 69

chai carrot cake 186

chai tea sauce 158

cheese: beet ravioli 67
    broccoli and pesto pizza 146
    broccoli soup and feta cream 24
    cauliflower crust pizza 149
    cottage cheese and horseradish dip 86
    croquettes with mustard mayo 165
    eggplant and red pepper lasagne 111
    endive and pear gratin 65
    goat's cheese and beet pizza 144
    gratin dauphinoise 58

green pea and broccoli fritters 41
    halloumi veggie skewers 150
    herbed beet, lentil and feta salad 90
    kale and mushroom pizza 144
    labneh 132
    rawmesan 28
    roasted ragù and pappardelle 112
    smoky sweet potato tahini pie 37
    Västerbotten pies 49
    whipped cheese 22
    zucchini involtini 27
    see also mascarpone

cheesecake, no-bake mango 182

cherry chutney 131

chia jam 154

chickpeas: chickpea and spinach curry 99
    classic hummus 34
    mini Caesar salad baskets 28
    salad in a jar 146
    sweet potatoes, kale and spicy
    chickpeas 75

chiles: chile sauces 7
    soy and chile dressing 79
    Västerbotten pies 49

Chinese cabbage: kimchi 109

chipotle jackfruit tacos 106

chocolate: black sesame ice cream 179
    chocolate and mascarpone cream 154
    chocolate cashew butter cream 70
    date and beet chocolate cake 70
    homemade chocolate spread 154
    midsummer dream cake 50
    orange tahini chocolate spread 176

chutney, cherry 131

citrus salad 64

coconut: potatoes serundeng 138

coconut cream: black sesame ice cream 179
    matcha coconut pannacotta 175
    whipped coconut cream 185

coconut milk 7
    cauliflower smoothie 76
    golden Kerala curry 96
    lemongrass and butternut squash soup 139
    sambal goreng buncis 126

coconut oil 7

coleslaw, winter 61

confit, blackberry onion 55

coriander pesto 139

cottage cheese and horseradish dip 86

couscous: Tunisian eggplant and pepper stew
    117

crêpes: green crêpe cake 154

crisps: hot eggplant 15

kale 15
sweet potato 15
croquettes with mustard
    mayo 165
crudités, rainbow 34
curry: chickpea and spinach curry 99
    curried flatbread pizza 30
    golden Kerala curry 96
    rainbow curry table 99

dates: date and beet
    chocolate cake 70
    no-bake mango cheesecake 182
    pumpkin seed and date cream 21
Dijon dressing 90
dill and horseradish cream 41
dips: ajvar 138
    almond sesame 168
    artichoke 34
    classic hummus 34
    cottage cheese and horseradish 86
    red pepper miso 15
    satay 18
dressings: Caesar 28
    Dijon 90
    lemon almond 75
    lemon and mustard 44
    lemongrass 87
    new moon 76
    soy and chile 79
    vinaigrette 64
    yogurt 117
drinks: golden milk latte 33
    mango lassi 33
    pink grapefruit margarita 33
    smoothies 76
    warm mulled apple juice 55

edamame beans: wabi-sabi salad 80
eggplants: ajvar dip 138
    caponata 171
    eggplant and red pepper lasagne 111
    eggplant kebab 153
    hot eggplant crisps 15
    miso-glazed eggplant 166
    roasted ragù and pappardelle 112
    Tunisian eggplant and pepper stew 117
eggs: bibimbap bowls 109
    garlic mushrooms and cavolo nero 104
    green garden salad 44
    smörgåstårta 47
endive and pear gratin 65

farmer's market and noodle salad 79
farro: pea farrotto 158
faux fishcakes 168
fennel chops, caramelised 160
fishcakes, faux 168
flatbreads: curried flatbread pizza 30
    Nordic nacho salad 86
flour, homemade gluten-free 149
freekeh: salad in a jar 146
fritters, green pea and broccoli 41
furikake 166
    hurricane furikake seasoning 12

garlic: garlic mushrooms and cavolo nero 104
    garlic sauce 153
    sweet garlic sauce 30
    yogurt lemon garlic sauce 135
ginger and hibiscus poached pears 180
gluten-free flour 149
goat's cheese: goat's cheese and beet
        pizza 144
    whipped cheese 22
golden Kerala curry 96
golden milk latte 33
grapefruit: pink grapefruit margarita 33
gratins: endive and pear
        gratin 65
    gratin dauphinoise 58
gravy: green peppercorn 56
    mushroom and shallot 69
green beans: sambal goreng buncis 126
green crêpe cake 154
green garden salad 44
green mash 163
green pea and broccoli fritters 41
green peppercorn gravy 56

halloumi veggie skewers 150
harissa: labneh and harissa
        roasted carrots 132
    roasted baby pumpkins stufffed with harissa
        lentils 115
hasselback celeriac roast 69
hazelnuts: homemade chocolate spread 154
herb and mustard rub 69
hibiscus tea: ginger and hibiscus poached
        pears 180
horseradish: cottage cheese and horseradish
        dip 86
    dill and horseradish cream 41
hot and smoky seitan bangers 163
hot sauces 7
hummus, classic 34

hurricane popcorn 12

ice cream, black sesame 179
icing: lime and rose 186
    mascarpone 50
Indian carrot salad 101

jackfruit: chipotle jackfruit tacos 106
    jackfruit bulgogi 125
    jackfruit bulgogi salad 89
jam, chia 154

kale: kale and mushroom pizza 144
    kale crisps 15
    sweet potatoes, kale and spicy chickpeas 75
    winter pesto sauce 67
kimchi 109
    bibimbap bowls 109
    kimchi fried rice 139

labneh and harissa-roasted carrots 132
lasagne, eggplant and red pepper 111
lassi, mango 33
latte, golden milk 33
leeks: gratin dauphinoise with roasted leeks 58
lemon: lemon almond dressing 75
    lemon and mustard dressing 44
    lemony cashew cream 15
    yogurt lemon garlic sauce 135
lemongrass: lemongrass and butternut squash
        soup 139
    lemongrass dressing 87
lentils: herbed beet, lentil and feta salad 90
    herbed lentil meatballs 56
    roasted baby pumpkins stuffed with harissa
        lentils 115
lettuce: mini Caesar salad baskets 28
lime and rose icing 186
lingonberry glaze 70

mangoes: mango lassi 33
    no-bake mango cheesecake 182
margarita, pink grapefruit 33
marinara sauce 143
mascarpone: chocolate and mascarpone
        cream 154
    eggplant and red pepper
        lasagne 111
    mascarpone icing 50
    midsummer dream cake 50
    smörgåstårta 47
matcha powder 175
    matcha coconut panna cotta 175

mayonnaise, mustard 163, 165
meatballs, herbed lentil 56
midsummer dream cake 50
milk: golden milk latte 33
    smoothies 76
mini Caesar salad baskets 28
mint avocado smoothie 76
miso 166
    miso-glazed eggplant 166
    miso wow sauce 83
    red pepper miso dip 15
    seared miso mushrooms 126
    tofu dengaku 125
mushrooms: bibimbap bowls 109
    garlic mushrooms and cavolo nero 104
    halloumi veggie skewers 150
    hot and smoky seitan bangers 163
    kale and mushroom pizza 144
    mushroom and shallot gravy 69
    Nordic nacho salad 86
    roasted ragù and pappardelle 112
    seared miso mushrooms 126
    smoky shiitake with pea farrotto 158
    wabi-sabi salad 80
mustard: Dijon dressing 90
    herb and mustard rub 69
    lemon and mustard dressing 44
    mustard mayonnaise 163, 165
    mustard soured cream sauce 42

new moon salad 76
no-bake mango cheesecake 182
noodles: farmer's market and noodle salad 79
    rainbow noodles 139
Nordic nacho salad 86
nori: furikake rice 166
    hurricane popcorn 12
nut milk: lemon almond dressing 75
    smoothies 76
nuts: homemade gluten-free flour 149
    no-bake mango cheesecake 182
    see also almonds, walnuts etc

okonomiyaki 11
onigiri 16
onions: the big roast! 135
    blackberry onion confit 55
    caponata 171
    caramelised onion tarte tatin 22
    halloumi veggie skewers 150
oranges: citrus salad 64
    orange tahini chocolate spread 176

pak choi with ginger and garlic 130
pancakes: green crêpe cake 154
    okonomiyaki 11
panna cotta, matcha coconut 175
pappardelle, roasted ragù and 112
parsnip fries 138
pasta: beet ravioli 67
    eggplant and red pepper lasagne 111
    roasted ragù and pappardelle 112
pastry, spelt 22, 37
pea shoots and zucchini salad 84
peanut butter: satay dip 18
pears: endive and pear gratin 65
    ginger and hibiscus poached pears 180
peas: green pea and broccoli fritters 41
    pea farrotto 158
peppers: ajvar dip 138
    the big roast! 135
    creamy red pepper sauce 150
    eggplant and red pepper lasagne 111
    halloumi veggie skewers 150
    rainbow salad 153
    red pepper miso dip 15
    roasted ragù and pappardelle 112
    summer rolls 18
    Tunisian eggplant and pepper stew 117
pesto: broccoli and pesto pizza 146
    coriander pesto 139
    winter pesto sauce 67
pickles: onigiri 16
    pickled veg 42
    tsukemono 129
pilaf 99
pine nuts: rawmesan 28
pink grapefruit margarita 33
pistachio nuts: winter pesto sauce 67
pizza: bake-your-own pizza party 143
    broccoli and pesto pizza 146
    cauliflower crust pizza 149
    curried flatbread pizza 30
    goat's cheese and beet pizza 144
    kale and mushroom pizza 144
    tahini, sweet potato and avocado pizza 144
polenta with caponata and roasted beets 171
pomegranate, seared Brussels sprouts with 64
popcorn, hurricane 12
potatoes: croquettes 165
    gratin dauphinoise 58
    new potatoes with dill and chives 42
    potatoes serundeng 138
    puffed potatoes 65
pumpkin: caramelised fennel chops with
    pumpkin purée 160

pumpkin, wild rice and lemongrass salad 87
    roasted baby pumpkins stuffed with harissa
        lentils 115
pumpkin seed and date cream 21

quinoa: new moon salad 76

radicchio: cherry chutney radicchio salad 131
    okonomiyaki 11
ragù and pappardelle 112
rainbow crudités 34
rainbow curry table 99
rainbow noodles 139
rainbow salad 153
raita 99
raspberries: chia jam 154
    midsummer dream cake 50
ravioli, beet 67
rawmesan 28
red cabbage: rainbow salad 153
    red cabbage cider confit 163
    summer rolls 18
    winter coleslaw 61
ribollita 103
rice: bibimbap bowls 109
    faux fishcakes 168
    garlic mushrooms and cavolo nero with
        red rice 104
    herbed lentil meatballs 56
    kimchi fried rice 139
    miso-glazed eggplant with furikake rice 166
    onigiri 16
    pilaf 99
    wabi-sabi salad 80
rillette, smoked tofu 44

salads: best tomato salad ever 138
    cherry chutney radicchio 131
    citrus 64
    farmer's market and noodle 79
    green garden 44
    herbed beet, lentil and feta 90
    Indian carrot 101
    jackfruit bulgogi 89
    mini Caesar salad baskets 28
    new moon 76
    Nordic nacho 86
    pea shoots and zucchini 84
    pumpkin, wild rice and lemongrass 87
    rainbow 153
    salad in a jar 146
    strawberry summer salad 93
    summer rolls 18

sweet potatoes, kale and spicy chickpeas 75
wabi-sabi 80
wakame 129
watermelon and Chioggia beet 83
watermelon buckwheat 150
winter coleslaw 61
salted caramel 185
sambal goreng buncis 126
satay dip 18
sauces: cashew tahini 61
  chai tea 158
  coriander pesto 139
  creamy red pepper 150
  garlic 153
  green peppercorn gravy 56
  marinara 143
  miso wow 83
  mushroom and shallot gravy 69
  mustard soured cream 42
  okonomiyaki 11
  red wine 160
  tahini 144
  wabi-sabi 80
  winter pesto 67
  yogurt lemon garlic 135
  *see also dips; dressings*
sausages: hot and smoky seitan bangers 163
seeds: homemade gluten-free flour 149
  *see also sesame seeds*
seitan sausages 163
sesame seeds: almond sesame dip 168
  black sesame ice cream 179
  crispy sesame broccoli 120
  furikake rice 166
  hurricane popcorn 12
shallots: mushroom and shallot gravy 69
shiitake with pea farrotto 158
skewers: eggplant kebab 153
  halloumi veggie skewers 150
smoothies: beet carrot 76
  cauliflower 76
  mint avocado 76
smörgåsbord 42
smörgåstårta 47
soups: broccoli soup and feta cream 24
  lemongrass and butternut squash soup 139
soured cream: mustard soured cream sauce 42
soy sauce 7
  soy and chile dressing 79
  wabi-sabi sauce 80
spelt flour: basic pizza dough 143
  midsummer dream cake 50
  spelt pastry 22, 37

spinach: cauliflower crust pizza 149
  chickpea and spinach curry 99
  green garden salad 44
  mint avocado smoothie 76
  Nordic nacho salad 86
  rainbow salad 153
squash *see* butternut squash
stew, Tunisian eggplant and pepper 117
strawberries: midsummer dream cake 50
  strawberry summer salad 93
summer rolls 18
sweet mess with salted caramel 185
sweet potatoes: smoky sweet potato tahini pie 37
  sweet potato crisps 15
  sweet potatoes, kale and spicy chickpeas 75
  tahini, sweet potato and avocado pizza 144
sweeteners 7

tabil spice mix 117
tacos, chipotle jackfruit 106
tahini: cashew tahini sauce 61
  classic hummus 34
  orange tahini chocolate spread 176
  smoky sweet potato tahini pie 37
  sweet tahini babka 176
  tahini, sweet potato and avocado pizza 144
  zesty tahini cream 115
tandoori cauliflower 101
tarts: caramelised onion tarte tatin 22
  smoky sweet potato tahini pie 37
  Västerbotten pies 49
tempeh, hot tamari 84
tequila: pink grapefruit margarita 33
tofu: farmer's market and noodle salad 79
  faux fishcakes 168
  smoked tofu rillette 44
  smörgåstårta 47
  tofu dengaku 125
  wabi-sabi salad 80
tomatoes: best tomato salad ever 138
  caponata 171
  eggplant and red pepper lasagne 111
  marinara sauce 143
  rainbow salad 153
  ribollita 103
  roasted ragù and pappardelle 112
  strawberry summer salad 93
  Tunisian eggplant and pepper stew 117
  zucchini involtini 27
tortillas: chipotle jackfruit tacos 106
  Nordic nacho salad 86
tsukemono 129
Tunisian eggplant and pepper stew 117

Västerbotten pies 49
vinaigrette 64

wabi-sabi salad 80
waffles 185
sweet mess with salted caramel 185
wakame salad 129
walnuts: creamy red pepper sauce 150
watermelon: watermelon and Chioggia
  beet 83
  watermelon buckwheat salad 150
whipped cheese 22
whipped coconut cream 185
wild rice: pumpkin, wild rice and lemongrass
  salad 87
wine: red wine sauce 160
winter coleslaw 61
winter pesto sauce 67

yeast, nutritional: herbed lentil meatballs 56
  rawmesan 28
yogurt: dill and horseradish cream 41
  feta cream 24
  labneh 132
  mango lassi 33
  simple raita 99
  sweet garlic sauce 30
  tandoori cauliflower 101
  yogurt dressing 117
  yogurt lemon garlic sauce 135

zucchinis: zucchini involtini 27
  pea shoots and zucchini salad 84

# Thanks

————

**To my family, Natal, Nova, and Evan, and to my table guests,** friends, and helpers, Santouscha Tjietaman, Bensimon Van Leyen, Sarah Cheikh, Fleur Schouten, Marie Sophie, Surf Avalon, Aïsha Zafirah, Geraldine Faureau, Paul Edouard Tastet, Tim Holdredge, Fabio Bortolazzi, Imogen Visscher, Djenna Wallace, Manu, Suzanne, Jessica, Q Oijjevarr, Jesse and Zanna Kalf, Willemijn Meijer, Yannick Steensma, Sam Hof, Haye Beeldman, Suze Boorsma, Ulysis, Tisha Prins, Kesia Jorissen, Ryan Oijjevaar, Bo Oijjevaar, Floris Schmidt, Franky Howe, Joris Perez, Silvan Arhem, Jaqueline Schouten, Juliette Kwikkers, Natalie Ilario, Jan, Barbara and Norbert van Leyen, Gerard Bouwman, and Thom Widdershoven.
An extra warm and special thanks to Olivia (@adelasterfoodtextures) for our Midsummer celebration on Bohusläns coast in Sweden, and to the Swedes: Alexandra Toftesjö, Moa Hallmyr Lewis, Maria Andreassen, Kristina Larsson, and Edward Thorden.
A special namaste to my sister Leoni and Sekoya Yoga and Holistic Center for the friendship through thick and thin, and not to forget for invaluable production assistance.
Warm thanks to Suus Slee from @foodbandits for lending props.

**Huge thanks to my editor, Sophie Allen,** and Sarah Kyle at Kyle Books for invaluable input and hard work with this book. Also to the copy editor Jo Richardson for translating my Swenglish (Swedish-tinted English) into flawless English.
And a big thanks to the talented production team for a beautiful finish on my photography.

**Also thanks to my readers and Instagram followers** for your invaluable support, feedback, and love. This book is for you! I never thought I would hear back from so many happy eaters after *Bowls of Goodness* was published, and it's now one of the reasons why I want to keep making and share recipes. It's truly a rewarding feeling, knowing that the food is cooked and enjoyed in homes all over the world. If you cook from this book and like to post your creation on social media, feel free to tag me and use the hashtag #feastsofveg. I can't wait to see it.

# Resources

————

My favorite set of ceramics, (frequently) used in this book, is handmade by AnneMieke Boots Ceramics. Find her at www.annemiekebootsceramics.nl or on Instagram @annemiekebootsceramics.

These are brands and creative friends whose products and services I relied on in the making of this book. Find them on Instagram or their homepages:
@foodbandits @cultchakombucha @organicfoodforyou
@tallyho_offical, @debiologischenordermaarkt @knead_more_bread
@organicfoodforyou @sekoyacenter @letoile.store